English Philosophy since 1900

G. J. WARNOCK

English Philosophy Since 1900

Second Edition

OXFORD UNIVERSITY PRESS
London   Oxford   New York
1969

Oxford University Press
OXFORD LONDON NEW YORK
GLASGOW TORONTO MELBOURNE WELLINGTON
CAPE TOWN SALISBURY IBADAN NAIROBI LUSAKA ADDIS ABABA
BOMBAY CALCUTTA MADRAS KARACHI LAHORE DACCA
KUALA LUMPUR SINGAPORE HONG KONG TOKYO

First published in the Home University Library *1958*
First issued as an Oxford University Press paperback *1966*
Second edition, first published as an Oxford University Press
paperback *1969*

PRINTED IN GREAT BRITAIN
BY RICHARD CLAY (THE CHAUCER PRESS) LTD
BUNGAY, SUFFOLK

Preface

THE TEXT WHICH FOLLOWS is a revised version of a book first published in 1958; and I should make clear first of all what revisions I have made. The major changes are three. First, the book originally contained a chapter called 'Logic', in which I attempted some discussion of the nature of logical systems and of their value and limitations in the treatment of philosophical problems. This chapter has been entirely removed, for two reasons. For one thing, I was aware at the time, and even more uncomfortably aware later, that what I had there produced was an extremely sketchy, superficial, and incomplete account of matters of great complexity and difficulty; a tolerable treatment of the questions raised would have been much longer, and the text as it stood seemed to me perhaps worse than useless. But further, in considering how that chapter might be made more viable, I came in fact to doubt its relevance; the use of formal systems as paradigms or tools in philosophical argument, though conspicuous in Russell, has not been characteristic of more recent English philosophy, so that it seemed to me unclear, in the context of this book, what use was supposed to be made of any conclusions that might be reached on that subject. Accordingly, I decided, with a certain relief, that the best course would be, not to attempt to improve that particular chapter, but to cut it out.

Secondly, I have written into the first chapter a few paragraphs about Cook Wilson and some of his followers. I have not said very much on this subject, since it still appears to me, as it did ten years ago, that the historical importance of this early brand of 'Oxford philosophy' is not very great. However, it has seemed to me wrong that it should not be mentioned at all, even in an admittedly selective historical account; and also there are in fact both certain resemblances and certain actual connections between Cook Wilson's 'school' and more recent, more conspicuous Oxford philosophers. There are, specifically, links between Prichard and Austin.

Thirdly, in the chapter called 'New Questions' I have put in some additional material about some of the work that has been done, or has become available, in the last ten years. In particular, since Austin's death in 1960 much of his most characteristic work, previously known only through his lectures, has appeared in print, and it seemed obviously proper that this should be rather more fully discussed than would have been practicable ten years ago.

Besides making these comparatively substantial changes, I have revised the Bibliography; I have added a number of notes in commentary on or correction of the text; and I have made a certain number of actual changes in the text, too numerous and really too minor to be separately specified. All footnotes, other than simple references, are new. There is a certain inescapable unsatisfactoriness in revising an existing text as I have tried to do; apart from the danger, which should be avoidable, of introducing actual muddles and inconsistencies of detail, there is the less palpable unsatisfactoriness of attaching passages composed from a present standpoint to a text written, inevitably with the passage of time, from a rather different one, and hence of fabricating perhaps a hybrid piece of work with no definite point of view at all. I hope, however, that I have amended too little to fall into this trap too grossly. This is not a new book; substantially, it remains an old one slightly altered, and so maintains, I hope, reasonably firmly the angle from which it was originally written. I have certainly not altered everything with which, now, I might be inclined to quarrel.

I would like now to say something about the book as a whole. I am afraid that, when it was first published, it was given a somewhat misleading title; I have been deterred from trying to devise a better one only by the certainty of making confusion worse confounded—it would surely be intolerable, and indeed almost fraudulent, to have substantially the same book in circulation under two different names. In any case, the fact is, and ought to

be emphasized, that this is not really a book about English philosophy since 1900; in it I make no attempt at the comparatively
complete, comprehensive historical account which such a title
might naturally lead one to look for. That what I have attempted
to do should be called what it really is not, merits apology; but
that it should be what it is, is at least reasonably explicable.

What this book really attempts to do, in its limited space, is to
make clear in brief outline how some very general philosophical
ideas have evolved, and in particular, perhaps, how the idea of
philosophy itself has changed, in the present century. The aim
was to include such detail as seemed necessary for this general
purpose and to leave out, by and large, what would have been
secondary or superfluous to it. No attempt is made even to mention, let alone to discuss, everything and everybody. Conspicuously, there is nothing in the pages that follow about recent
writings in ethics and political theory—not of course because they
are no good or of no interest, but because, as it has seemed to me,
work in those fields is not particularly well suited to the aim of
illustrating the general trend and character of philosophical development; large-scale shifts in the philosophical landscape are
more naturally, and more clearly, brought out by the consideration of philosophical work in less specialized fields. Perhaps
equally conspicuously, there are many good, recent and contemporary philosophers not mentioned in this book—and for the
same reason, namely, that there are many philosophers of merit
whose work, while meritorious, is not well adapted for my purpose
of illustrating rather general tendencies and trends. They would
have to come into a detailed historical narrative—such a narrative
as, for example, Professor Passmore admirably provides in his
monumental and invaluable *A Hundred Years of Philosophy*
(1957). But this book could not aspire to be monumental, and so
could not afford even to try to be comparably all-inclusive. Omis-
sion from its pages does not imply disrespect, and I trust that those
omitted will bear that in mind.

One further matter. In my Preface of ten years ago, in pointing
out, perhaps too cursorily, that I had been highly selective in
deciding who and what should be discussed, I ventured to make
the claim that, though judgement on such matters is fallible and
always disputable, 'the sketch of the landscape given here is not
an eccentric one'. Predictably, at least one critic has rebuked me

for saying this, and has charged that eccentric is exactly what it is. This is not the place, nor am I the person, to debate the merits of this charge, but perhaps I should mention what I take to be its grounds. I may be wrong about this, but I believe that some philosophers would maintain that my account is distorted in assigning too much importance to Moore and too little to Russell. There are, perhaps, two issues here. It might be held that, by comparison with Russell's prodigious fertility, intelligence, inventiveness, and technical sophistication, the achievement of Moore must look relatively minor; and it might be held, rather differently, either that it is not true that (as I suggest) historically Moore made 'more difference' than Russell, or even that the influence of Moore's patient, prosaic plainness was positively bad in its devotion to (perhaps) tedious detail. Historical judgement is likely to be influenced here by one's views as to the direction in which philosophy *should* have gone or be going; the question what was important in the past is not detachable from the question what is to be valued now or in the future. But in any case these are, I believe, issues with regard to which some would hold my picture to be wrongly drawn; and without conceding the charge of actual eccentricity, I should like to draw attention to this possible line of criticism.

Finally, to repeat what I said ten years ago, it goes without saying, of course, that in a book of this size compression and simplification in some degree have been necessary everywhere. But fortunately no reader of this book need have much difficulty in checking against the original documents, all of which are readily accessible, the account of the state of philosophy that is here submitted. Being fully aware that such accounts are no substitute for the real thing, I have included at the end of the text a short list of the most relevant articles and books, to which readers of the pages that follow are earnestly referred.

Contents

1

The Point of Departure

I N 1 9 2 4 A N D 1 9 2 5 there appeared two bulky volumes with the general title *Contemporary British Philosophy*. They make strange reading today. Their title itself, even then, was doubtfully appropriate. For the philosophical landscape which, in their own odd way, these books illuminate is that of a period some years earlier than their dates of publication. The essays of which they consist were written for the most part by philosophers who were already veterans, and the few contributions by younger men stand out most awkwardly among their venerable companions. The editor of the two volumes, J. H. Muirhead, expressed his belief that British philosophy had been brought back 'into the main stream of European thought', and added the hope that 'the present generation' would remain and prosper in that stream as he conceived it.[1] This hope, as the work of his younger contributors might well have led him to suspect, was doomed to almost immediate extinction. It might have seemed reasonable enough in, say, 1900; but it should have been clear by 1925 that the scene had changed, was changing, and would continue to change.

This transformation, though its early stages appear to have eluded the notice of Muirhead, has become by now a sufficiently conspicuous fact. It has been often remarked upon, sometimes with satisfaction, sometimes with lamentation and dismay. It has almost as often been misunderstood. It has been said to have generated a kind of 'revolutionary illusion', through which neither its friends nor its enemies can see the case clearly. It stands, in fact, in need of explanation. To attempt to explain exhaustively

[1] op. cit., First Series, p. 323.

why there occurred the changes that did occur would be an enterprise both ill-defined and, for the present at least, over-ambitious; but it ought to be possible to make at least reasonably clear what sort of transformation it is that we have to deal with.

Over Muirhead's two volumes of 'contemporary' British philosophy there broods the conspicuous presence of F. H. Bradley. Bradley was at that time too old to be represented in them in his own person. But he is mentioned in the preface as 'by general acknowledgement the foremost figure in British philosophy (perhaps in the philosophy of our time in any country) for the last generation'; and indeed very many of the essays that follow bear the marks of his doctrines, of his manner of thought, and of his style of writing. Another large presence is that of Bernard Bosanquet. Of these two H. J. Paton has recently written[1] that 'in their day and generation they were big men'; for philosophers generally they were 'the dominant figures even to those who opposed them'. The dominant doctrine which these big men represented, and which formed for many years the pervasive atmosphere of philosophy, has been called Absolute Idealism—in Paton's words, 'Hegelianism modified by Anglo-Saxon caution'. It was almost inevitable that philosophers of that period, even those of whom it would now seem difficult to believe, at some stage or other should all have thought of themselves as Hegelians of this modified variety. The chief architects of change, Bertrand Russell and G. E. Moore, though the stage in their cases was decidedly a brief one, were not exceptions to the general rule.

It would be extremely difficult to say what this species of philosophy exactly was. Perhaps indeed it was nothing at all exactly. It will be enough to say here in broad terms what it was like. It was in the first place highly and ambitiously metaphysical. The claim was made, that is, to establish striking and important conclusions about the universe as a whole, about Reality, not in this or that more or less superficial or limited aspect, but in its ultimate nature. The philosopher's concern with 'the whole' was constantly and powerfully contrasted with the merely partial or fragmentary interests of other disciplines; his endeavour to arrive at really 'ultimate' truths was distinguished from, say, scientific attempts to establish propositions that would serve for

[1] *Contemporary British Philosophy*, Third Series, Allen and Unwin, Macmillan, 1956, p. 343.

some non-ultimate purpose, or would satisfy some more or less arbitrary or provisional standard. It was held that what passed for truths in the world, or in the laboratory, were all, or almost all, somehow unsatisfactory—that for the philosopher there was not only something more, but also something very different, to be said.

The motives underlying these high endeavours were various, and not always explicitly avowed. It appears that Bradley was impelled by a dissatisfaction, which he himself half admitted to be not wholly intellectual, with all common and current ways of thinking and speaking. His discontent was a very fundamental one. We are all inclined to take it for granted, whatever our special interests, if any, may be, that the universe contains or consists of a number of things—that this unremarkable and rather un-informative proposition is surely as true as anything could be. But it appears to have been just this proposition which Bradley detested. It seemed to him to carry with it a view of the universe as a mere plurality of items; as fragmentary, disjointed, and ir-rational; as infected throughout with what most displeased him —namely 'bare conjuction'. It seemed to him that 'reason' could not tolerate such a view of the universe as this. He therefore set himself to show, with vast and indeed valuable ingenuity, that everything which, on this fundamental assumption, is taken to be real or true is, in an odd sense of his own, self-contradictory—is therefore to be condemned as 'mere appearance', as quite alien to the ultimate nature of Reality. Reality is to be found only in the Absolute, which neither is nor contains a number of things; in which all separation is overcome, all distinctions vanish, all seem-ing individuals and their apparent relations are merged; in which, in short, there remains no hint of any bare conjunction.

The motives of Bosanquet were in part rather different from this. He shared with Bradley the conviction that only the Abso-lute, 'the whole', was entirely satisfactory; he shared his small regard for ordinary ways of thinking. But he was influenced also, as Bradley was not much, by the hope of discovering some ulti-mate, unshakeable basis for ethics, or more generally some sort of guarantee for all judgements of value. If, he explained, we 'experience the positive quality of the absolute', then 'the intrinsic connection of reality and value becomes here transparent to us'.[1]

[1] *Contemporary British Philosophy*, First Series, p. 72.

We see that 'totality expresses itself in value'. J. E. McTaggart, a rather younger Cambridge philosopher who zealously shared in the general deference to Hegel, was even more candid as to his practical interest. 'The utility of Metaphysics is to be found,' he said, 'in the comfort it can give us'—'in the chance that it may answer this supreme question (whether good or evil predominates in the universe) in a cheerful manner, that it may provide some solution which shall be a consolation and an encouragement.'[1] However, whereas Bosanquet and many of his contemporaries were inclined to the view that philosophy might sometimes justify and even demand positive social or political action, McTaggart seems rather to have thought that 'comfort' was enough. If we found that the universe was a fairly cheerful place, there was not much that we could do to make it more cheerful still.

It is not surprising that a philosophy of this variety—so ambitious, so deliberately un-ordinary, so determinedly grave—should have found expression in a characteristic manner of writing; and indeed it is probably the change in this respect which would strike most immediately a reader who compared the philosophy of fifty years ago with that of today. If he were attached to the presently prevailing mode, and had the courage of his convictions, he might well find the style of the Idealists almost unbearable.[2] It had at its best an undeniable splendour. Bradley in particular was capable of impressive rhetoric, and conveys quite often in his extraordinary sentences a sense of explosive intellectual energy. Bosanquet's manner was less idiosyncratic but more literary than Bradley's, and closer to bombast. He wrote sometimes with an air of vague high seriousness, in which the serious intent was almost completely muffled by the vagueness. And in the writings of the lesser men solemnity and unclarity seem to rise not seldom to the pitch of actual fraud. But it is necessary to be careful in framing, if one wishes to frame, a complaint about this state of affairs. It might seem the merest truism to say that, if argument is to be carried on, rhetorical figures, stylistic variation, and literary high colour can only be distressing impediments: and it was precisely on his superior logical acumen and argumentative rigour that the Idealist metaphysician was most apt to insist.

[1] *Philosophical Studies*, pp. 184, 151.
[2] An exception should really be made here of McTaggart, whose way of going on had both the merits and the defects suggested by the term 'scholastic'.

If so, it might seem reasonable to object that his prose was a medium most ill-suited to the display of his talents; inflation of language is almost always irritating, but it positively frustrates the close exposition of an argument. However, it may be that this objection would be misplaced. It may be, as Bradley would presumably have wished it to be, that there was an 'intrinsic' and not merely fortuitous relation between Idealist thought and the usual style of its expression. Bradley's opinions perhaps, whatever his claims may have been, were not strictly susceptible of demonstration, but depended, among the relatively unimportant trappings of argument, mainly upon the persuasive force and artifice of their presentation. If so, to strip off the highly coloured rhetorical dress would be to harm substantially the doctrine itself, or even to find that one arrived, as with an onion, at nothing in the end. The Idealists could hardly have been expected to do this for themselves.

The movement of philosophy away from this prevailing atmosphere has often been represented, usually by hostile critics, as a break with tradition.[1] We are sometimes told not only that British (or English-speaking) philosophy of the recent past is not what philosophy used to be, which no doubt is to be expected, but that it is something of a quite different sort from what it had been by long tradition; it is implied that this must merit concern or even dismay. In this idea there is, as we shall find, not no truth at all, but there is in it also a measure of historical falsehood. It is true that philosophy in the manner of Bosanquet and Bradley has, in defiance of the forecasts of J. H. Muirhead, declined to a condition very nearly approaching non-existence; but it is not true that philosophy in that manner was ever, in this country, the usual or traditional thing. On the contrary, the state of British philosophy in the early years of the present century was itself highly unusual and full of novelty. It bred, no doubt, its own revolutionary illusions. To see in it now a tradition is

---

[1] Some critics have claimed to detect in this and the following paragraphs, and have deplored, some hint of philosophical chauvinism, of Idealism's being condemned as the brain-child of sinister foreigners. This was not my intention. It is true that, in the late nineteenth century, the main influence on philosophers in this country was continental in origin; but my point was not, of course, that this was a bad thing, but that it was a somewhat unusual thing. The historical point is scarcely deniable, and need not be confused with any judgement of value.

certainly a mistake. It may possibly have been, as Muirhead twenty years later thought that it still was, in 'the main stream of European thought'. But it is unquestionable that it had not been there for very long, and that the main stream of British thought had run for some centuries in very different channels.

This was clear enough to a foreign observer. The Italian De Ruggiero, whose *Modern Philosophy* was published in 1912, was of the opinion that 'the speculative level reached by English Idealism' was high. But he saw clearly that this then dominant mode of thought was still very new in British philosophy, and he confessed himself unable to explain how his British contemporaries had done, as he thought, so well in so short a time. He suggested some connection with the Romantic revival. He mentioned the names of Coleridge, Wordsworth, Carlyle, and Ruskin. He alluded to the stimulus of late Victorian agnosticism, so exasperating to 'a religious race like the English'. But the start of the strictly philosophical movement could be dated exactly, he held, from the publication in 1865 of J. H. Stirling's *The Secret of Hegel*. There is indeed much evidence to suggest that it was in fact at about this time that 'German Idealism began to find a home in British universities'. English and Scottish philosophers may have started late in this particular race, but their fervour very rapidly made up for their comparative tardiness. It has been said that they expressed 'the vital spirit of an era'. If an era may be measured in intensity and not only in duration the remark is not quite wholly absurd.

However, it is clearly very far from being the case that the brand of philosophy from which reaction was so soon to occur was in England time-hallowed and venerably traditional. It was in fact an exotic in the English scene, the product of a quite recent revolution in ways of thought due primarily to German influences. Bertrand Russell, a major cause of the exotic's demise, was the god-son of John Stuart Mill, 'so far as is possible in a non-religious sense',[1] and he thus symbolically joins hands with at least two centuries of British philosophy, across a gap of a few years occupied with new and strange things. Of course, the fact that Absolute Idealism was a recent and very much an alien import does not entail that it deserved the extinction which overtook it. But to think of it as *traditional* is to imply on its behalf a claim

[1] *The Philosophy of Bertrand Russell*, p. 3.

to respect to which it is not entitled. Conversely, to regard Moore and Russell merely as innovators is to forget that there exists, far removed from what they opposed, another lengthy tradition with which they are quite firmly connected. Hume or Berkeley would have been sadly puzzled by the pages of Bradley, to say nothing of Hegel's. But either might have conversed quite naturally with Moore, and with Russell too, at least in his less technical moments.

Nor should the extent of the reaction led by Russell and Moore be exaggerated. They were not at first, and perhaps they never were, opposed in general to metaphysics. Moore said in 1910 that 'the most important and interesting thing which philosophers have tried to do' is to give 'a general description of the *whole* of the Universe';[1] and this, the characteristic metaphysical aim, he certainly did not consider to be in principle vicious or impossible. Russell announced in 1918 his own intention of setting forth 'a certain kind of metaphysic',[2] and he believed that this could be attempted with good prospects of success. He intended to replace Absolute Idealism with a *different* system of metaphysics; while Moore, who had no system of his own, was for the most part engrossed in trying to establish to his own satisfaction the meaning of, and the grounds for, the many surprising things which Idealist and other philosophers had said. He did not think they had said nothing, or that what they had said could not possibly be true. The idea that metaphysics is in principle impossible, or 'meaningless', did not appear until many years later, at a time when, in this country at least, old-style Idealism was already moribund; and even then, it was an idea which neither Russell nor Moore either sponsored or accepted.

It would also, I believe, be historically improper to give the impression that Idealism perished of *refutation*. It is true that some of Bradley's fundamental views, such as his doctrine of 'internal relations' or his theory of truth, were subjected to destructive criticism. But metaphysical systems do not yield, as a rule, to frontal attack. Their odd property of being demonstrable only, so to speak, from within confers on them also a high resistance to attack from outside. The onslaughts of critics to whom, as likely as not, their strange tenets are very nearly unintelligible

[1] *Some Main Problems of Philosophy*, p. 1.
[2] *The Philosophy of Logical Atomism*: see *Logic and Knowledge*, ed. Marsh, 1956, p. 178.

are apt to seem, to those entrenched inside, misdirected or irrelevant. Such systems are more vulnerable to *ennui* than to disproof. They are citadels, much shot at perhaps but never taken by storm, which are quietly discovered one day to be no longer inhabited. The way in which an influential philosopher may undermine the empire of his predecessors consists, one may say, chiefly in his providing his contemporaries with other interests. In the present case the old spells were broken, and a new spell was cast, chiefly by reason of the character of G. E. Moore.

However, before turning to that matter, some notice should be taken of another kind of 'resistance movement', centred in Oxford, and roughly contemporary there with both the heyday and the subsequent decline of Idealism. Here the leading figure—earnest, vigorous, and impressive, but also elusive and curiously easy to overlook—was that of John Cook Wilson. He held the chair of Logic at Oxford from 1899 to 1914, and locally at least his reputation stood very high as a gifted teacher and formidable controversialist. There is a sense in which it would be true to say that he and his disciples have left almost no traces in contemporary philosophy. The actual course of philosophical development reveals in retrospect a certain irony in the withering contempt with which Cook Wilson regarded the logical writings of 'B. Russell' (as he always called him); and H. W. B. Joseph, in certain respects a follower of Cook Wilson, was not much more fortunate in 1932-4, when he conducted in the pages of *Mind* a ferocious controversy on logical topics against the pro-Russell advocacy of Susan Stebbing. This was indeed a case in which Oxford appeared, at any rate at the time, as the home of lost causes. There are, however, interesting connections to be traced at least between the manner and interests of the Cook Wilson 'school' and the manner and interests of later and more conspicuous Oxford philosophers.

Cook Wilson never wrote a book.[1] This may have been, in part, because of his temperament; fierce and contentious though he was (he himself confessed to an excessive love of dialectical

---

[1] His lectures, papers, and philosophical correspondence were published after his death, in 1926, in two volumes entitled *Statement and Inference*, with a memoir by A. S. L. Farquharson.

triumph), he was not really self-confident, and perhaps disliked the idea of committing himself too much at large. But also his way of thinking was not such as naturally to issue in thick volumes. He had no broad theory about the nature of things in the Idealist manner, and was not interested enough in theories of that kind even to wish to argue at length against them. His concern was with philosophical (not, emphatically, with formal) logic; and even here his most strongly held doctrines were in a sense negative, so that his natural mode was that of piecemeal criticism of particular theses advanced by others. This trait was even more marked in H. A. Prichard, perhaps his ablest and most important follower, whose bent of mind was undeviatingly destructive, and whose conclusion in argument seems often to have been that, except by way of refutation, there is practically nothing to be said on any philosophical subject.

What Cook Wilson meant by 'logic' might, less misleadingly to a modern reader, be called the theory of knowledge, but for the awkward point that he strenuously insisted that there could be no such thing. The logician's interest in what he is apt to call 'statements' is, of course, Cook Wilson held, not an interest in certain verbal expressions. Not that verbal expression is unimportant; indeed, distinctions observed in grammar and in 'ordinary usage' were regarded as respectfully by Cook Wilson as by Aristotle long before, and J. L. Austin soon afterwards. Still, verbal expressions are not the subject-matter of logic. Many would bring in here the idea of 'propositions' which verbal expressions propound; but Cook Wilson's interest was drawn in another direction by opposition to the Idealist orthodoxy of his day. The Idealist logician said that logic had to do with *judgement*, and from this Cook Wilson vigorously dissented.

He took the Idealists' talk about judgement to imply, whether or not this is what they actually intended, that, when anything is seriously said in the statemental mode, something is 'judged'—that there is an act of the mind called *judging* which occurs in any such case, producing a *judgement* expressible in the linguistic dress of a statement. Now judging, he held, does indeed occur; my judgement may be, for example, that the dollar is likely to be devalued before the end of 1970, and I may express my judgement in that form of words. But this, it is clear, is a particular case, not the general case; *judging* that the dollar is likely to be devalued is not *supposing* that it will be, nor is it knowing, or taking for granted, or merely entertaining the idea. To 'judge' is really to make an inference or appraisal from certain evidence, or on certain grounds, that one has; and one is not always doing this when one speaks in the indicative mood. There are different cases; it is important to seek to understand how they differ; and in so far as the Idealists implied that there was some single mental act which is *invariably* what statements give expression to, they were radically mistaken. There is no such thing.

The most interesting case, Cook Wilson naturally supposed, is the case of knowing; for this is in a sense the goal, or ideal, to which believing, inferring, supposing, and the rest aspire; knowing is, so to speak, what they all would be, if they could. We are inclined to ask, then, what knowing is; but it is essential to realize, Cook Wilson and Prichard both constantly insisted, that there is no possible answer to this question. It is in this sense that they held, as a cardinal point of doctrine, that there can be no such thing as 'theory of knowledge'. Regrettably, but clearly, they were mistaken in holding this; to say what knowing is is certainly very difficult, but it is not impossible. Why should it be? A notion so evidently complex as that of knowledge seems unlikely to be insusceptible of analytic definition. And if their point was, as sometimes it seems to have been, that any purported 'justification' of knowledge cannot but be circular, then, in the first place, this is not the same as the allegation that knowledge is not definable, nor, in the second place, does it appear to be true in any very interesting sense. It may be true that one who doubts whether anything at all can be known cannot have his doubt allayed by argument; for there will be nothing to which any argument could appeal, which he would not regard as already itself put in question by his general doubt. But it does not follow, as Cook Wilson and Prichard seem to imply that it does, that there is no sense in seeking justification, ever, for particular knowledge-claims. It is true that what might justify a particular knowledge-claim must be something else supposed itself to be known. But why not? When we question whether something in particular is known to be the case we are not usually questioning whether anything is known at all, nor is there any ordinary reason why we should wish to do so. The trouble arises, perhaps, from the supposition that knowing is, as judging and the rest were supposed to be, a 'mental act'; for if knowing were some particular mental act one might think that one who performs it must know straight off that he does so, and further, that if he questions in any case whether he really does perform it, his questioning must at once become both general and interminable—since the *same* 'mental act' would occur in any instance of knowing, doubt in any one instance must at once infect every instance. And so, since on this view doubt could never be removed, perhaps it was thought vital to insist that it must never be admitted—one must insist, in Prichard's words, that 'when we know, we know that we know', and must decline any further argument on the subject.

This mistake about knowing, this insistence that there is really nothing to be said about it, was both unfortunate and damaging —damaging in that it made it too easy for its proponents, most conspicuously for Prichard, themselves to issue startlingly dogmatic knowledge-claims for which no credentials were felt to be necessary, or even possible. (This propensity, in ethics, is perhaps at the root of that fervent but almost aphasic 'intuitionism' of which Prichard was the most extreme exponent.) But historically it was important that this group of philosophers continued, markedly in contrast with the practice of Idealism, a style of detailed, laborious examination of particular points, largely though not wholly without doctrinal presuppositions, and with a kind of Aristotelian regard for common ways of speaking and for ordinary beliefs. They wrote without eloquence; they believed firmly in the utility of detailed argument, at least where they believed that there was room for arguments to be deployed. It is true that their writings are, in a sense, peculiarly baffling. Cook Wilson's, as already mentioned, are both fragmentary and some-what negative—nor, it may be added, internally consistent; in Prichard also we find, again mostly in posthumous volumes, a mass of detailed argument, many changes of opinion, and no clear general picture—notably, no clear indication of what sort of subject he took philosophy to be, what sort of results he supposed philosophical argument might yield, or what sort of thing the 'solution' of a problem would be. This is baffling, certainly, but admirable in a way; one feels that Prichard was quite ready to accept *anything* which seemed to him to be the conclusion of a cogent argument, and, if often enough this led him to accept conclusions which may now seem scarcely sane, at least it is patently serious—he is not manipulating things in the interests of preconceived doctrine, not seeking to impress with rhetoric, not stacking the cards.

The link between Cook Wilson and much later Oxford philosophy runs through Prichard. There is, first, the quite general point that it was Prichard by whom, in his undergraduate days, J. L. Austin was most impressed, and to whom (with Moore) he must have owed something of his own preference for small points, plain diction, slow progress, and detailed argument. The taste for high doctrine was not to be acquired from that source; and if, as has been mentioned, Prichard offered no clear picture of what sort of subject philosophy is, Austin came to regard this as a virtue rather than a defect—to hold that the picture cannot be clear because the subject is itself such a tangle, and that general views about the nature of philosophy are liable to function as blinkering preconceptions.

But there is, second, a more detailed point of connection than this. In the later 1930s Prichard was much preoccupied with the problem of what it is to make a promise. Austin corresponded with him at some length on this subject, and it was from this correspondence, as he himself recorded, that he was eventually led to the notion of a 'performative utterance', thence to the more general notion of a 'speech-act', and so to perhaps his most important and much later contributions to the philosophy of language. The link here is not, of course, doctrinal; it is a connection, partly of interest in a particular topic, but perhaps more importantly in attitude of mind. The preference for taking one point at a time, the distaste for eloquence, the mistrust of generalization and large doctrine, the freedom from prejudice—these qualities of Austin's, sometimes ascribed on the strength of his example to 'Oxford philosophy' in general since 1945, were in some degree inherited from those earlier, less notorious 'Oxford philosophers' who worked in uneasy, sometimes contentious cohabitation with the statelier exponents of Absolute Idealism.

2
G. E. Moore

I SAID IN THE last chapter that, among the immediately operative factors contributing to the decay of Absolute Idealism, special
notice should be paid to the *character* of Moore. The word may
have seemed, perhaps, curiously chosen; but it was chosen
deliberately. For it was not solely by reason of his intellectual
gifts that Moore differed so greatly from his immediate predecessors, or influenced so powerfully his own contemporaries. He was
not, and never had the least idea that he was, a much cleverer
man than McTaggart, for example, or Bradley. It was in point of
character that he was different, and importantly so. He seems to
have been, in the first place, entirely without any of the motives
that tend to make a metaphysician. He was neither discontented
with nor puzzled by the ordinary beliefs of plain men and plain
scientists. He had no leanings whatever towards paradox and peculiarity of opinion. He had no particular religious or other cosmic
anxieties; and he seems to have felt that in aesthetics and morality
(not, of course, in moral or aesthetic *philosophy*) all was as well,
at least, as could reasonably be expected. He thus did not hanker
for any system on his own account. But secondly, he had the
great force of character that was necessary to resist the temptation
to conform himself with his environment. He soon overcame, if he
ever had, the desire so natural in any clever young man, to excel
in the same line of business as his admired elders. He did not
borrow a modish metaphysical idiom to make up for, or to conceal, his own real lack of relish for any such thing. And thirdly,
he seems never to have had the slightest difficulty in causing his
views to be taken seriously. It was always clear that his opinions,

however unorthodox or naïve they may have been or seemed, were not those of one who could safely be disregarded.

The character of his original interest in philosophy was both very simple and, in its context, strikingly original. He went to Cambridge in 1892 to read classics, hardly aware at that time 'that there was such a subject as philosophy'. But the encouragement of, among others, Bertrand Russell first engaged his interest in philosophical discussions, and then led him, at the end of his first year, to start reading philosophy. His concern with the subject was, in a sense, indirect. 'I do not think that the world or the sciences would ever have suggested to me any philosophical problems. What has suggested philosophical problems to me is things which other philosophers have said about the world or the sciences.'[1] In discussions at Cambridge he heard propositions asserted to which he could attach no clear meaning, and he sought to have it explained what their meaning was. He heard things asserted which he could see no sufficient reason to believe, and he tried to find out on what grounds the assertions were made. It appeared to him that his companions sometimes denied what every sane man knew quite well to be true, and he made patient efforts to persuade them that they ought not to do this. McTaggart on one occasion 'had been led to express his well-known view that Time is unreal. This must have seemed to me then (as it still does) a perfectly monstrous proposition, and I did my best to argue against it. I don't suppose I argued at all well; but I think I was persistent.'[1] No doubt he was.

The most striking feature of his philosophical questioning was, perhaps, its very simplicity and directness. His mind always worked most naturally in concrete terms. If Time is unreal, ought we not to deny that we have breakfast *before* we have lunch? If Reality is spiritual, does it not follow that 'chairs and tables are far more like us than we think'? Can it really be doubtful whether material objects exist, since it is certain that here is one hand and here is another? Moore did not in every case wish to suggest that the strange things philosophers said were certainly untrue. But he did wish to make it quite plain that they were very strange. He wished to point out how astonishing were their implications. He wanted to have it understood how

---

[1] *The Philosophy of G. E. Moore*, p. 14.

much work was to be done, if grounds were to be offered that
would really require their acceptance. In all of this he was neither
obstinate nor disingenuous. He was not less well able to follow an
intricate argument than were the philosophers he questioned; he
was far more exacting in his standards of clarity and rigour. His
puzzlement, indeed his bewilderment, at the things they were
willing to assert was entirely sincere. He was gradually driven to
the disturbing conclusion that an enormous amount of philosophical writing was marred and frustrated by *hastiness* and *confusion*. Philosophers, it seemed to him, were fatally addicted to
embarking on the search for answers to important-seeming questions without considering *exactly* what questions they were trying
to answer. They were liable, too, to make one or two points in an
argument, and forthwith to consider their whole question as
closed. But often, even usually, these points could be shown to be,
however impeccable in themselves, entirely inadequate as grounds
for the conclusion supposedly based on them. If the conclusion
was, as conclusions were by no means always, clear, it might be
obvious enough that the question whether it was true or false
was exceedingly interesting. 'Reality', for example, 'may be
spiritual, for all I know; and I devoutly hope it is.' That opinion
at least is 'truly interesting and important'. But one must realize
how very *different* the opinion is from what any ordinary person
believes; how *many* propositions must be disproved and proved
before it could possibly be said to be established; what a vast
number of arguments must, therefore, be involved; and how remote we are, really, from any position in which we would see the
doctrine to be true or, alternatively, false. The usual starting-
point for Moore's early work was something which seemed to him
to be, if not a 'perfectly monstrous proposition', at least a very
strange and surprising proposition; and his 'method', if indeed he
can be said to have had any such thing, was simply to raise, with
regard to its meaning and its grounds, any question he could
think of that seemed to him to be in need of an answer. He found
that such questions were numerous enough to provide him with
plenty of hard work.

The effect, in the highly elaborated and refined atmosphere of
Idealism in the 1890s, of the appearance of such a simple, direct,
pertinacious inquirer can easily be imagined. It was supposedly
agreed on all hands that quite ordinary opinions were quite

certainly defective; that common ways of speaking were almost always unsatisfactory; and that *therefore* it was quite clearly imperative to devise new ways of speaking, new and subtler opinions, in order to withstand the close scrutiny of philosophical criticism. There was doubtless no agreement as to what particular refinements were called for, or exactly what paradoxes they were that should be boldly embraced; but there was no disposition to question the general view that very many very common opinions must be ruthlessly rejected. Moore struck in fact, though perhaps unwittingly, at the very foundations of all the current philosophical structures. He asked, in effect, why they were *needed*. What exactly was supposed to be wrong with very ordinary opinions? Why exactly were common ways of speaking to be condemned? So far from being disposed to assume that beliefs very widely held were very probably mistaken, he was inclined to suppose that they were almost certain to be true. If not, exactly why not? And if some other opinion were put forward as being an improvement, what was it exactly, and how was it thought to be established? For some people at least, the mere raising of such questions as these—the mere refusal to submit without question to Idealist spells—had apparently the force of a liberation. The emperor was seen to have, if not quite no clothes, at least not very many. Russell himself has said that Moore's influence worked upon him as an 'emancipation';[1] it proved possible to walk out of the intellectual prison as soon as a simple, open-eyed inspection was made of its walls. Why should one try to believe that Time is not real? There was quite suddenly seen to be no reason at all.[2]

What, then, if one abandoned the aim of constructing paradoxical alleged improvements upon, or corrections of, people's ordinary opinions, was left for the philosopher to do? There remained, of course, the considerable task of unravelling the pronouncements of other philosophers; and to this Moore himself devoted a great deal of attention. But he did not think, or at least did not think for very long, that this was the only sort of task for philosophers to undertake. There was also the task which he called 'analysis'. Here we must turn to some actual examples.

[1] *The Philosophy of Bertrand Russell*, p. 12.
[2] This does not mean, of course, that Time is completely unproblematic. Moore's point was, I think, only that, whatever McTaggart's arguments might establish, they *could* not sensibly be taken to establish what he *said*.

In 1925 Moore published an article called 'A Defence of Common Sense'.[1] It begins with a list of what he calls 'truisms'—such as that he has a body, was born a certain number of years ago, has lived since that time on or near the surface of the earth, which itself had existed for many years before he was born, and on which live and have lived very many other human beings. Every one of these propositions, Moore says, 'I *know*, with certainty, to be true.' They are all *wholly* true; their meaning is in no way doubtful or obscure; and Moore knows also that very many other people know vastly many truths of a sort similar to these. However, he observes that a great many philosophers have made assertions apparently incompatible with these truisms. They have asserted that there are no material things at all, that Time is unreal, that perhaps there exist no minds other than their own; and in some cases at least, Moore believes, they have used such words as these in such a way as really to contradict some or all of his truisms. At the same time, it is quite certain that they knew those truisms to be true. For even in their philosophical writings they have alluded to themselves, and to other philosophers, or to possible readers, in such a way as to reveal their knowledge of the existence of themselves and of other people, and of the ordinary world in which they and others were living. The chief peculiarity of Moore's own position is, he says, that while he shares with all other philosophers the knowledge that what may be called 'the Common Sense view of the world' is, in certain fundamental respects, wholly true, he does not *also* hold, as they have often done, views inconsistent with that view of the world. 'But this difference seems to me to be an important one.'

But, he goes on to say, he does not mean to imply that there are no questions for serious dispute. For although, with regard to all his truisms, it would be 'quite certainly the height of absurdity' to wonder whether they are true, or whether we know this, it is no less certainly quite proper to wonder what is the correct *analysis* of them. Indeed, 'no philosopher, hitherto, has succeeded in suggesting an analysis of them, as regards certain important points, which comes anywhere near to being certainly true'. It is not, as some philosophers appear to have thought, that their analysis is clear but their truth uncertain. The case is exactly the

---

[1] *Contemporary British Philosophy*, Second Series, pp. 193–223,

reverse of this. Their truth is absolutely certain, but their analysis is doubtful.

Some years later, in 1939, Moore discussed[1] the observation of Kant that, if anyone expresses doubt of the existence of 'things outside us', 'we are unable to counter his doubts by any satisfactory proof'. Moore first examines with very great care the meaning of the expression 'things outside us'. He decides that, though there may be some things as to which it is doubtful whether they should be so called, yet there are very many things that would, if they existed, certainly be of the kind in question—as, for instance, dogs, planets, stars, shadows, and hands. He then offers a proof that there do exist things outside us. 'Here is one hand,' he says, 'and here is another'; therefore, at least two things outside us exist; and one could add as many other such proofs as might be required. The premises here are quite certainly true, and the conclusion quite certainly follows from the premises. There is no doubt, he says, that the proof is 'perfectly conclusive'. Once again, however, he is careful to make the admission that the *analysis*, both of the premises and the conclusion, is more than doubtful. It is proper to wonder how such propositions ought to be analysed; the absurdity consists only in wondering whether they are true, in supposing that they are not known, or that they cannot be proved.

Before raising the question what Moore means here by 'analysis', we ought to take notice of the baffled astonishment which both of these papers are liable to generate. Are they not, one is tempted to protest, altogether too simple? Can it really be that many philosophers have held opinions rather obviously incompatible with what they themselves and others knew to be true? Can it be that Kant did not know that he had two hands, or did not see that hands fell under the heading of 'things outside us'? Can it really be to the point to insist that certain propositions are true, which are in fact just what Moore calls them—that is, truisms? Surely there must be more to it than this. But what more?

Attempts have been made to bring out the point of Moore's procedure, and hence to remove the sense of baffled astonishment, by supposing that he slightly misstated his case. It has been sug-

[1] *Proof of an External World*, Hertz Annual Philosophical Lecture. London, Humphrey Milford.

gested[1] that he was really concerned with the defence, not of
Common Sense, but of *ordinary language*. Suppose it to be agreed,
as it naturally would be, that there frequently arise situations in
which, if someone were to say 'This is a hand', it would by all
ordinary standards, and taking the words in their ordinary sense,
be admitted that what he said was true, and that he knew what
he said was true. Now it might perhaps be urged that there are
other standards, and other senses of the words, according to which
what he said was *not* true, or at least he did not know it to be true;
and some philosophers might wish to maintain that these other
standards and senses were *correct*, in opposition to those that we
all ordinarily employ. Moore's point, on this interpretation,
would then be that it does not make sense, when discussing an
expression in ordinary language, to argue thus that its ordinary
employment is *not correct*. For what could be the correct way of
employing it, if not the way in which it is ordinarily employed by
those who know the language in question? Moreover, when Moore
produces his cases of ordinary things that we (therefore) can correctly say, we all feel at once how perfectly correct they are, and
how absurd it is for any philosopher to condemn such a way of
speaking. 'The philosophizing of most of the more important
philosophers has consisted in their more or less subtly repudiating
ordinary language. Moore's philosophizing has consisted mostly
in his refuting the repudiators of ordinary language.'[2]

Now this interpretation of Moore's intentions certainly makes
sense of much that he said, and attributes to him a species of argument that is, within certain definable limits, both salutary and
entirely sound.[3] But I do not think one can say that Moore
actually had any such intentions. Most of the reason for this is
that Moore was quite exceptionally careful always to say exactly

---

[1] e.g. by Malcolm, in *The Philosophy of G. E. Moore*, pp. 345–68. Malcolm
has subsequently retracted some points in his argument.

[2] Malcolm, loc. cit., p. 365.

[3] I should like to emphasize that there are limits. It has been suggested
that this kind of argument could once have been used to prove the existence of
witches, since 'witch' was at one time a term well established in ordinary
language'. Well, any form of argument can be foolishly misapplied. Rather
similarly, Moore's 'defence of Common Sense' could be read, very foolishly, as
a defence of absolutely anything that is widely believed. Moore himself did not
offer a definition of 'Common Sense', except in terms of the particular propositions which he discussed.

what he meant; but what he actually said is not at all what he is thus represented as having meant. The fact is that he does not anywhere express the idea that ordinary language is *ipso facto* correct, nor does he argue against other philosophers for attempting, overtly or covertly, to alter it. He always presents the case quite differently. What he defends is always the *truth* of certain very common propositions, and not the propriety of the language in which they are expressed; and he takes the view that other philosophers have held doctrines incompatible with the *truth* of these propositions, not that they have merely rejected the common use of words. That much philosophy has consisted in 'more or less subtly repudiating ordinary language' is a *theory* about philosophical theories, to which Moore has at least never committed himself. He seems, on the contrary, always to have taken the more direct view that philosophers were seeking to arrive at the truth, can be supposed to have meant what they said, and hence to have seriously taken to be true what their words would naturally be taken to mean. He does indeed, in a sense, 'defend ordinary language'; but only, I think, in the sense that he regards it as adequate for our purposes, and considers that technical or other unusual ways of speaking are often more dangerous than beneficial. Much more important than this, in his own view, is surely the defence of the *truth* of common-sense *statements*—the insistence that (however difficult their analysis may be) no philosophical argument whatever could show them to be false, or even doubtful.

If, then, we cannot say that Moore himself believed that other philosophers were engaged in 'repudiating ordinary language', what did he consider that they were doing? How did he account for the extraordinary fact that, as he says, they frequently asserted doctrines incompatible with what they themselves knew to be true? Philosophy, one might think, must be a most peculiar subject, if this is what philosophers so often are led to; but what does the peculiarity consist in? I believe that Moore never had a general answer to this question. He certainly believed that philosophers were often confused and often argued invalidly, and thus were often led into making assertions that were unclear, or false, or unfounded. But to the question why in particular these assertions so often had the air of paradox, of running counter to our very simplest convictions, he seems to me to have had no answer to give. It is one of the chief merits of his work that it raises this question clearly and sharply; the unshakeable ordinariness of his own assertions makes us most keenly aware of the extreme oddness of the views he objected to; but he does not tell us what exact sort of oddness it is. He believes that his opponents have argued badly; but in that, by itself, there is nothing particularly odd. He would perhaps have suggested, though this is not certain, that other philosophers had commonly failed to distinguish between debating the truth or falsehood of a proposition, and debating the question of its correct analysis. Perhaps sometimes, entangled in the quite genuine difficulties of analysing even some very simple proposition, they had been betrayed by defects of clarity into believing the truth of the proposition to be in question. But in fact he seems commonly to have rested in the straightforward belief that philosophers, through confusion or fallacy or both, were apt to say things that were quite clearly untrue; that whatever the reasons may have been for this odd state of affairs, it was essential first to insist that the plain truths they questioned or denied were true; and that then it was proper to raise, in a comparatively clear atmosphere, the question how these truths ought to be *analysed*.

What, then, was involved in this notion of analysis? The problem of giving an analysis of a proposition was thought to be, in a sense, just the problem of saying what the proposition *meant*. One might be inclined to object at once that, if so, the task of analysis ought not to be so very laborious as Moore both says, and by his practice often seems to show, that it is—for do we not all, by his own admission, already know the meanings of the sorts of propositions he considers? However, a first reply to this objection would be that, though certainly we all do know what is meant by, for instance, the proposition that this is a hand—though we all do understand the sentence 'This is a hand', as one who did not know English would not understand it—yet we may not be able, without careful thought, to *say* what it means. To know how to use a form of words correctly is one thing; to be able to say how we use it is quite another. Part of the difficulty, then, in giving correct analyses may consist in the difficulty simply of saying quite clearly what it is that some phrase or proposition, whose meaning is probably not in doubt, does actually mean.

But Moore found the problem of giving analyses to be difficult,

at least in many cases, for reasons other than this. In fact, he involved himself in some trivial embarrassments by laying down
conditions that any successful analysis must satisfy, which un-
luckily are partly too stringent, and partly too vague, for any
analysis on those conditions to turn out successfully. But these
minor difficulties can be fairly easily eliminated. At least two
serious ones remain.

   In the first place, Moore took very seriously a suggestion that is
implicit in his metaphorical name for his enterprise. The use of
the word 'analysis' carries the suggestion that something complex,
something constructed, is to be decomposed—that its component
elements or parts are to be distinguished, and its mode of construction from these elements or parts made clear. Now there are
certainly some cases in which it is natural enough to think of propositions in terms of this seductive metaphor. A cube, for example, can be thought of naturally enough as a geometrical
complex of planes in three dimensions; the proposition 'This is a
cube' seems likely, accordingly, to be susceptible of analysis in
terms of these planes, their number, their shapes, their mutual
relations. It is arguable, no doubt, how exactly the analysis should
go; but one would naturally suppose that it must work out in
some not impossibly complicated way. But now what of the proposition 'This is a hand'? Is the notion of *being a hand* absolutely
simple, a notion so basic and elementary as to be in principle in-
capable of any analysis? It hardly seems quite so simple as that.
But if not, what elements are they into which it can be analysed?
What entities are they that are simpler, more basic, than hands,
of which hands could be said to be, in some strange sense, con-
structed or composed? Moore had no doubt that there were
simpler entities of some sort, on which our knowledge of hands
(and of other such things) was in some way based, and which
were indeed what we always directly referred to in uttering such
propositions as that this is a hand. But certainly these entities have
no familiar name, nor are we (in spite of our apparently incessant
direct acquaintance with them) ourselves familiar with any such
entities. Moore employed for referring to them the technical term
'sense-data'. He then seemed to be faced with two serious difficulties—first, that of making quite clear the meaning and use of this
invented expression; and second, that of seeing how by its employment such propositions as 'This is a hand' ought to be analysed.

We know, perhaps, how people are related to crowds or how plane squares are related to cubes; but how are sense-data related to hands? What *are* sense-data? Moore seems to have believed that analysis of almost any of his common-sense truisms led at once to questions about sense-data, and these questions he found so extremely difficult that, in spite of constantly repeated efforts, he never believed that he had finally answered them. It was as if, in pursuit of these analyses, he always found himself falling out of the bottom of ordinary language, and never at ease with the invented language which he thought was called for in that predicament.[1]

Secondly—though this is not a quite separate point—Moore involved both himself and others in difficulties resulting from the unquestioned assumption that any analysis must be of a standard pattern. It was always to consist in providing a verbal paraphrase of what was to be analysed, in the form of a longer, more explicit, but strictly synonymous phrase or sentence. A favourite and significantly simple example was the analysis of 'x is a brother' into 'x is a male sibling'. But the fact is that very many of our words and phrases are not thus tightly related to any more explicit synonyms, and can be made to seem to be so only by artificial devices. It is also true, and not less important, that this sort of analysis may sometimes leave out exactly what is of most philosophical interest. Consider, for instance, Moore's struggles with the concept of *goodness*. He believed this concept to be unanalysable—rightly, perhaps, in his own terms, since the function 'x is good' may not be usefully susceptible of more explicit synonymous paraphrase. But instead of regarding this point as being, what in fact it is, wholly uninteresting, and transferring his attention accordingly to the quite subtle and important ways in which, and purposes for which, the word 'good' is used, Moore evidently concluded that there was nothing more to be said. Goodness was simply unanalysable; and because it shared this quite uninterest-

---

[1] This suggests, what I think is true, that there was in Moore's conception of analysis a strong epistemological strain. The question, of what elements a given complex was composed, was taken to be at least very closely related to the question, what are the actual grounds, or foundations, of our assertions and claims to knowledge about items of that kind; ideally, the 'direction' of analysis would be towards a supposed epistemological ground-floor. Analysis in this sense is, of course, a very old-established feature of the 'empiricist' tradition, and is conspicuous also, as will be seen, in the work of Russell.

ing property with, for example, yellowness, he was able to assume that goodness and yellowness were somehow *alike*. 'Good' and 'yellow', he thought, were both names of simple qualities. The very great and important differences between the uses of these two adjectives appear to have escaped his notice altogether, in consequence of the fact that they do not lie where he was predisposed to look for them; that is, they cannot be made to emerge within the pattern of an analysis conceived so rigidly as Moore conceived it. The constricting effect of this rigid conception could be shown in almost any number of similar examples.

What can be said, then, of the general effect of Moore's work? We have taken note already of the very powerful impact of his good sense, simplicity, directness, and argumentative rigour upon the china-shop of Idealism. For the rest I believe there is divergence between his theory, so far as he ever had one, and his actual practice. In theory he seems never to have abandoned the idea that the goal of philosophical inquiry is to establish very general truths about the world—even, perhaps, about Reality as a whole. He believed no doubt that such truths, if any such were established, would not be at all so strange and surprising as his predecessors had held, and even hoped, that they would be; for he did not conceive of the possibility that 'the Common Sense view of the world' might prove to be untrue. Still, in theory he did not conceive of philosophy quite differently from his metaphysical predecessors. His practice, however, consisting as it mostly did in the pursuit of analyses, naturally tended to give rise to the idea that the business of philosophy is clarification and not discovery; that its concern is with meaning, not with truth; that its subject-matter is our thought or language, rather than facts. In its influence the practice was far more important than the theory. It is curious that just the same is true of his contemporary Russell.

3
Bertrand Russell

SINCE THE VERY BEGINNING of the present century Bertrand Russell has been so fertile in ideas, and so prolific of words, that there must be both great difficulty, and great injustice, in reducing his work to the measure of our present inquiry. He probably disliked Idealism more intensely than Moore did, partly perhaps because he was less blankly immune to its fascination. He has certainly proclaimed, both more explicitly and more often, more numerous alternatives to its procedures and objectives. We must select for attention the most conspicuous of these, and consider first what his relevant predispositions were.

In the first place, Russell had been as an undergraduate a mathematician, and he soon became also a logician of a highly professional sort, the master and to some extent the inventor of new and newly rigorous techniques. He seems very early to have felt, with justice, that by contrast with his own work and that of a few others in logic and the philosophy of mathematics, the writings of most contemporary philosophers were exceedingly loose, amateurish, and obscure. He was fond of saying that philosophy ought to be, as it had never yet been, 'scientific'—not only not less rigorous and exact, but more so, than mathematics and the physical sciences. It is perhaps not true to say that Bradley and the rest had made no attempt to come up to this austere standard; but it could scarcely be held that they had succeeded very well. Accordingly Russell felt a strong desire to bring into philosophy some sort of professionalism, some technique, which would enable the subject genuinely to bear comparison with such patronized, supposedly inferior disciplines as those of the scientist and the mathematician. His insistence upon this point—his propaganda almost—was certainly of very great value in retaining for, and in some degree restoring to, philosophy the charms of intellectual respectability.

Secondly, Russell was suspicious, again with justice, of the fact that most metaphysicians obtained, and some deliberately sought, satisfaction from the theories that they devised. This seemed to him, again, to be grossly 'unscientific'. It appeared that the results of philosophical inquiry were at least allowed, if not actually intended, to be influenced by the needs and wishes of the inquirer —that for instance McTaggart's 'cheerful' conclusions were esteemed in part at least for the comfort they offered, and not solely because they appeared on investigation to be true. Against this he set up—with, it must be confessed, occasional flights of romantic rhetoric on his own part—the scientific ideal of an entirely neutral, disinterested inquiry, altogether unswayed by such irrelevant factors as a desire for consolation, by religious beliefs, or by moral convictions. The philosopher's aim, as he wrote in 1914, should be 'to give an account of the world of science and daily life'. In the pursuit of this aim he should employ the most rigorous methods of logic, and not be distracted in any way by his personal needs or wishes or extraneous beliefs. The method to be followed should be that of *analysis*. Bradley, with his extreme distaste for 'bare conjunction', his insistence that Reality must really be a seamless, undifferentiated whole, had of course insisted that analysis involves falsification, that it can only lead us to unintelligible fragments, and hence is the very opposite of the route to truth. Russell scarcely troubled to argue against this. Remarking pointedly that many philosophers were 'less anxious to understand the world of science and daily life than to convict it of unreality in the interests of a suprasensible real world', he simply dissented from Bradley's opinion and embarked upon his own ambitious analytic programme.

There are of course enormously many different things that might be called 'giving an account' of the world of science and daily life. The sort of account which Russell intended to give was, as he explicitly admitted, metaphysical. The question 'What is there in the world, and what is it like?' was not to be given any obvious answer, such as a haphazard, empirically collected catalogue of things would provide. The question was to be answered much more generally and more fundamentally. The aim was to strip off the surface complexities of the world, and so to arrive at and isolate 'the last residue in analysis'; and what is to be found at this point of no further reduction will not be objects of any ordinary and familiar kind. Unlike Moore, Russell was willing and indeed markedly eager to emphasize that his findings would be very curious and surprising. He would never have dreamed of defending Common Sense; he would almost have judged it a denial of philosophy to do so. What philosophy had to reckon with, in Russell's opinion, was not Common Sense, but science. The philosopher's reconstruction of the world out of the elements located by his analyses need not comprise everything imputed to the world in everyday language and opinion, but must be adequate to the formulation of definite scientific knowledge. It need not, and indeed would not, look familiar and ordinary to ordinary men. 'The point of philosophy is to start with something so simple as not to seem worth stating, and to end with something so paradoxical that no one will believe it.'[1] Mathematics and science after all held plenty of surprises; surely it was proper that philosophy should hold some as well.

First, then, what is it that Russell proposes to analyse? The answer, a surprising one perhaps, is *facts*, not things. 'The things in the world have various properties, and stand in various relations to each other. That they have these properties and relations are *facts*, and the things and their qualities or relations are quite clearly in some sense or other components of the facts that they have those qualities or relations. The analysis of apparently complex *things* . . . can be reduced by various means, to the analysis of facts which are apparently about those things. Therefore it is with the analysis of *facts* that one's consideration of the problem of complexity must begin.'[2] Facts, since they have components, must be in some sense complex, and hence must be susceptible of analysis.

Facts are stated in propositions, and propositions in turn are complex; they are put together, made up of *words*. Some words, however, are simple. Consider the word 'red', for example. It seems quite obvious that our understanding of this word is not a complex resultant of anything yet simpler; in this case understanding can only be achieved by acquaintance with what it is that the word 'red' symbolizes, that is, a particular shade of colour. The word 'red' is thus not capable of analysis, and may be said to be a simple symbol. It is, in particular, a simple *predicate*. Contrasted with simple symbols of this sort, there must be simple symbols of another sort, namely *proper names*—the words, that is, by which we can refer to the particular things to which predicates are ascribed. The simplest sort of proposition, then, will be one which consists solely of a proper name and a simple predicate. This sort of proposition Russell calls 'atomic'; and the facts that such propositions state are atomic facts.

Now it is easy to see that out of atomic propositions we can construct more complex propositions. We can, for example, simply join two or more atomic propositions together with the words 'and' or 'or'. What we thus arrive at Russell calls a *molecular* proposition. But there are, as he holds, no molecular *facts*. Consider, for example, the molecular proposition 'This is red and that is brown'; what would make this true, if it were true, would not be one molecular fact, but rather the two atomic facts, that this is red, and that is brown. Molecular propositions are thus said to be 'truth-functions' of atomic propositions. That is, their truth or falsity is solely dependent upon the truth or falsity of the atomic propositions of which they are composed. Hence, though we need to have atomic facts to determine the truth or falsity of atomic propositions, we do not *also* require molecular facts.

So far, so good. But from this point on Russell found himself compelled to say things from which many of his followers sharply dissented, and which remained for some years as centres of controversy. In the first place, he held that there must be *general* facts, not only singular atomic facts. Consider the proposition 'All cats are black'. This cannot be said to be merely a conjunction of propositions, meaning 'This cat is black and that cat is black and . . .', and so on until all cats have been enumerated; for even if all cats *could* be enumerated, it would still be necessary to say in the end that the cats thus enumerated were all the cats there were; and here the element of generality has reappeared. What makes 'All cats are black' true or false, therefore, cannot be a conjunction of singular facts, but must be an irreducibly general fact. Next, he held also that there must be *negative* facts, since the truth or falsity of negative propositions could not otherwise be satisfactorily accounted for. And lastly, he accepted a peculiar species of facts corresponding to such propositions as 'Jones believes that the world is flat', or 'Smith hopes that the sun will be shining tomorrow'. The trouble here is that, although these propositions look complex, they cannot be said to be molecular in the sense explained above. The truth of 'This is red and that is brown' obviously depends in part on the truth of 'That is brown'; but the truth of 'Jones believes that the world is flat' is entirely independent of the truth of 'The world is flat'. For whether this is true or false, Jones may believe it. Hence, it is at least not clear that this sort of proposition is a truth-function of atomic propositions; and hence Russell felt obliged to admit that atomic facts alone were insufficient to make clear in what the truth or falsity of such propositions consisted.

It is not necessary now to go into the attempts that were made to dispense with these additional species of facts. Wittgenstein, Ramsey, Wisdom, and Russell himself all made great efforts from time to time to eliminate them. But at present the important point to apprehend is that they all shared a single ambition—the ambition, that is, of establishing the thesis that there were in reality only atomic facts, and in language only atomic and molecular propositions. These 'atoms', linguistic or factual, were the final, or the nearest approach to the final, 'residue in analysis'. They laid bare the essential character of language and of the world.

What made this ambitious metaphysical thesis seem plausible? Two factors can be disinguished here. In the first place, it had a kind of consistency with what had been, before the incursion of German Idealism, the most constant and perhaps the most fertile enterprise in which British philosophers had been engaged since the time of Locke. It had long been regarded as at least an important part of the philosopher's task to analyse the gross and complex constituents of human experience into their simplest elements; and it had always been assumed that to do this was to achieve a closer grasp of the facts, to learn something of the true nature of reality. The motives behind this enterprise had been admittedly various. Berkeley, for example, was fundamentally concerned to establish a peculiar sort of ontology, to show that we need not and indeed could not suppose the existence of anything but 'spirits' and 'ideas'; he was metaphysically opposed to metaphysical materialism. Hume on the other hand had been more neutrally interested in working out a completely thorough-going empiricism—in effecting 'reductions' wherever possible to the basic data of sense-experience. These philosophers tended to speak of words and 'ideas', where Russell would speak rather of propositions and facts; they proceeded also, by comparison with Russell, in a loose, informal, untechnical manner. But there is no doubt that in adopting the general aim of arriving at the simple by analysis of the complex, Russell and his followers were continu-ing a tradition which had long been familiar and seemed un-problematic.

But secondly, Russell was influenced more immediately by recent developments in logic, for which he himself had been in large part responsible. In his and Whitehead's *Principia Mathe-matica*, which was in a sense the culmination of work substantially initiated by Frege, he had devised a notation in which, as they sought to establish, it was possible to state not only the whole of logic, but also the whole of mathematics. The claim as to mathe-matics can be here disregarded, though it was of course of extreme importance in itself. What is of immediate relevance is the form that this notation took. It was explicitly truth-functional. That is to say, even the most elaborate formulae stateable in it were con-structed out of a few very simple forms, in such a way that the truth or falsehood of the formulae depended solely upon the truth or falsehood of these simple forms. Theoretically, as Russell often insisted, the complex formulae were all of them superfluous; they could all be construed as mere abbreviations of other expressions, often doubtless very lengthy, in which there would occur propo-sitions only of the simplest form, and one or two logical words such as 'and', 'or', and 'not'—theoretically, only one such word was held to be necessary. Now Russell often spoke of this notation as constituting a 'logically perfect language',[1] or at least as being intended to do this. Of course, as set forth in his book it had no vocabulary; there, the pursuit of complete generality had required the use of variables only, not particular words; but it included, he thought, at least the *syntax* of a perfect language. How then was this framework of a perfect language related to the sort of language we commonly employ? Here Russell appears simply to

[1] See, e.g. *Logic and Knowledge*, p. 198.

have assumed that it *was* the language we commonly employ, as
that would look if removable imperfections were removed; that is,
that his notation embodied the *essence* of language, and that
where languages differed or common language appeared to div-
erge, it was merely that this essential skeleton was concealed. It was
for this reason that the enormous assumption was made that all
propositions whatever which do not themselves state simple facts
must be truth-functions of those which do. Something like this
was manifestly true of the 'perfect' language, and hence it was
assumed to be true, though covertly of course, of any language
whatever.

It ought to be observed that these two factors—the trend of
the old analytic tradition, and the influence of new developments
in logic—did not point entirely to the same conclusion. If one
were influenced mainly by logic, there would seem to be no particular reason, except a desire for tidiness, to try to establish that
the necessary primitive, non-derived propositions were all of one
and only one sort. If Russell felt that general propositions must be
admitted as well as singular propositions, logic would furnish no
very strong motive for objecting to that view. But if one were
impelled by, for instance, a Hume-like desire to arrive at the basic
elements of sense-experience, to establish, that is, a general
empiricist thesis, one would then have a motive for wishing to
maintain that the *only* non-derived propositions were those which
recorded the occurrence of particular sense-data. The combination of these would lead, as it did lead, to the attempt to maintain
that singular atomic facts were really the *only* facts, and that *all*
propositions were either atomic or molecular.[1] This thesis appeared to have the double virtue of reviving pre-Idealistic empiricism, and of applying to philosophy the well-proved and dazzling
procedures of logic.

It ought by now to be clear enough why Russell said of himself
that he offered a 'metaphysic'. He was, in the first place, clearly
propounding an ontological doctrine—telling us, that is, what
'ultimately', 'in the final analysis', exists in the Universe. Furthermore, this doctrine was obviously not an empirical one. It was
arrived at substantially as a deduction, from a non-empirical
analysis of language, to the nature of that reality which language
describes. But it was a metaphysical theory of a peculiar, though

[1] cf. Urmson, *Philosophical Analysis*, pp. 95–7.

not perhaps a wholly new, variety. If one considers the theories of Bradley and McTaggart, one soon comes to feel, as Russell had felt with such deep disapproval, that an important purpose the theories were to serve was that of giving satisfaction to their pro-pounders. The same is fairly obviously true of Berkeley's. But it is not in any obvious way true of Hume's; nor is it true of Russell's. No doubt it may have yielded him intellectual satisfaction, but it neither had nor was intended to have any emotional, or religious, or moral implications whatever. For this reason it is rather diffi-cult to feel towards it as one would towards some more typical metaphysical theory. However, when one is told that reality can be in principle *completely* described in statements of the form 'This is red'—or even, on a more thoroughgoing view, of the form 'This that'—it is clear enough that something very strange is being said or implied about reality. There is no mistaking the metaphysical tone.

We must next observe a most curious fact—a fact which forms a kind of paradoxical link between Russell and his supposed anti-thesis, Bradley. It had sometimes been objected against Bradley that his own theory was suicidal. His insistence on the satisfactori-ness only of 'the Whole', on the non-contradictory nature only of the Absolute, seemed to imply 'the necessary falsity of every state-able truth'—that the only really acceptable statement would be one which stated everything simultaneously, but which of course cannot possibly be made. But if so, the assertions of which his own books consist must fall under this universal condemnation; if true, they themselves cannot possibly be true. It was soon pointed out in a similar spirit that the doctrines of Logical Atomism, if they were true, could not be stated.

This was the very singular conclusion of Wittgenstein's *Trac-tatus Logico-Philosophicus*, a work of impressive subtlety and power which presents difficulties of interpretation not less than, and indeed very similar to, those sometimes presented by a sacred text. The argument was this. According to the purest doctrines of Logical Atomism, a proposition can be stated significantly *either* if there is, or could be, an atomic fact to which it corresponds, *or* if it is a truth-function, however complex, of propositions of that sort. But most of the propositions which Logical Atomists, in-cluding Wittgenstein himself, purported to assert were not of either of these kinds. For these propositions mostly did not *state* facts; they purported rather to say something *about* facts, in particular about the relations between facts and propositions. But according to the theory itself such propositions cannot be significant; they purport to say what cannot possibly be said. Thus, Wittgenstein was led to, and heroically drew, the conclusion that most of what he himself had said was senseless; in an odd way, to understand his own book was to see that this was so, and to realize that, although perhaps he had succeeded in *revealing* something, he had not really *said* anything at all. This thesis, laid quite early like a sort of time-bomb in the basement of Logical Atomism, escaped notice, or was nervously disregarded, for a number of years; when it went off, its inventor and fortunately many others had already transferred themselves to other premises.

It ought to be said here that it would be a gross injustice to suppose that Russell's work had been of importance *only* in that he was the chief expositor of Logical Atomism. That aspect of his work has been singled out for attention on the ground that it was the most influential, and perhaps also the most characteristic, of its many sides and stages. But, quite apart from his eminence as a logician, Russell has also written on an immense range of philosophical topics, never without effect. Where so much is done, very much must inevitably be passed over; but it must not be forgotten.

4

Logical Positivism

CONTEMPORARY WITH THE MIDDLE and later stages of the
work of Russell and Moore was the movement well known as
Logical Positivism. The slightly political suggestion in the word
'movement' is not inappropriate since, for a time at any rate, the
philosophers of this group had much of the deliberate cohesion of
a political party, and even a definite programme, platform, or
creed. Their work at one time attracted a very great deal of attention; at least its existence, and something of its general character,
was known in much wider circles than ever took cognizance of the
work of Moore, or even of Russell. Their main thesis at least appeared, both to their friends and their enemies, to be immediately
intelligible; if stated polemically, as it very often was, it appeared
to be of very great importance; and in this country it had the
advantage of being presented with almost hypnotic clarity and
force in A. J. Ayer's *Language, Truth, and Logic*.[1] All this pub-
licity has been rather misleading. The name 'Logical Positivists',
once put into general circulation, has shown an obstinate tendency to stay there, and to be repeatedly misapplied with ever-
increasing inappropriateness. More seriously, it is probably true
to say that, partly because of its notoriety, too much has been
claimed for the movement itself, both for good and for ill. The
variety of metaphysical writing against which it was most vehemently directed was already languishing, if not quite dead, by the
time that the movement was well under way; and its undoubtedly
high standards of clarity and rigour were no longer new; they
had already been set, if not surpassed, by Russell and Moore and

[1] Gollancz, 1936; second edition, 1946.

their followers. The movement did probably make some salutary impression on minds unshaken by the milder impact of Russell and Moore. But to regard it as even mainly responsible for the near extinction of old-style metaphysics is to make, I believe, an error of history. That enemy was almost dead when the battle began.

The main features of the so-called Vienna Circle, from which Logical Positivism originated, were two: on the one hand an extreme respect for science and mathematics, and on the other an extreme distaste for metaphysics. Its main aim, which it is important to bear in mind, was thus to devise some clear criterion by the use of which science and mathematics would be proved acceptable, and metaphysics by contrast would be condemned. The Logical Positivists were not, as philosophers, concerned with the truth or falsehood of scientific statements; for this they held, rightly, to be the affair of the scientists. Their proper concern, as philosophers, was held to be with *meaning*. Accordingly, the criterion they devised was to be a test of meaningfulness or significance, a test which the sciences would pass and metaphysics would not. This criterion became known as the Verification Principle; and most of the literature of Logical Positivism is concerned with the formulation, always disputed, of this principle, and with the application of it in its various forms. Leaving aside the tangled disputes over its proper formulation, we can say roughly that what the principle laid down was this: first, that a statement is meaningful, means something, only if there is a way in which it could be verified (or 'tested'); and second, less importantly perhaps, that *what* a statement means is shown by, or somehow consists in, the method of its verification—it being assumed that verification must always at least terminate in empirical observation, or sense-experience. A special exception was made in favour of such analytic formulae as those of logic and mathematics, which do not require to be empirically verified at all. But the alleged statements of metaphysicians, theologians, or other such persons were held, in as much as they could not be empirically verified, to be condemned by the principle to mere non-significance.

This principle has a number of curious and interesting features. Perhaps the most curious is this—that it is easy, though misleading, to represent it as startlingly radical and (admirably or deplorably) destructive; and that it is also easy, though again misleading, to represent it as wholly innocuous and almost a triviality. Suppose first of all that we regard it as laying down a really *general* criterion of significance—that is, in such a way that anything at all which fails by this test is to be declared to be meaningless. It then appears at once that not only metaphysics, not only theology, but also every single moral and aesthetic judgement, any judgement of value of any sort, must be regarded as meaningless. For it seems clear that nothing that we say in any of these fields can be verified solely by empirical observation. If seen in this light— and indeed it was sometimes presented in this light—the Positivist thesis looks terrifyingly iconoclastic. It appears that not only a few venerable theorists, but almost all of us, are being charged with constantly uttering or writing down words which have, un- realized by us, no meaning at all. But suppose next that we regard the principle differently; suppose that we remind ourselves that it began with the words 'A *statement* is meaningful . . .'. We may then say that all that the principle really implies is that, if some utterance is not verifiable by empirical observation, then that utterance is not a statement. And surely in this there is no harm at all. All that it really requires us to do is to reserve the appella- tion 'statement' for those of our utterances which are empirically verifiable, and to call the others by other names; and to do this leaves everything substantially just as it was. Another way of reaching much the same result would be to regard the principle as formulating a criterion only for a certain kind of meaningfulness, say 'cognitive' meaning. What fails to satisfy the criterion could then be regarded either as condemned, if 'cognitive' meaning is the only respectable kind, or as substantially unscathed, if there are viable varieties of meaning other than the 'cognitive'.

But both these attitudes are in some degree misleading. It is certainly true that the first, most startling interpretation is mainly the product of misunderstanding. For it at least ought to have been clear from the first that the Verification Principle could have no application at all to forms of words which in no way aspired to the condition of statements. It does not make sense to speak of the verification of commands, prayers, promises, expressions of wishes, and so on; these accordingly do not *fail* to be verifiable; and to say of them that they cannot be verified is to make a some- what trivial remark which in no way impugns their linguistic respectability, and of course in no way implies that they are meaningless. The *general* conclusion, then, that non-satisfaction of the verification principle at once implied the verdict 'meaningless' was always a foolish misunderstanding. However, the principle can hardly be regarded, in the manner of our second interpretation, as utterly innocuous. It is after all by no means arbitrary what we call a 'statement' and what we do not; it is not a mere matter of free linguistic choice. Similarly, what does or does not have 'cognitive' meaning could scarcely be a purely trivial, verbal question; it is a question on which issues of some real substance depend. To say a prayer, we would all agree, is not usually, or at least not merely, to make a statement. But to utter a moral judgement is a good deal more like making a statement; and some might well feel that something would be lost in a view which flatly declared that a moral judgement could *not* be a statement. And more seriously, are there not some propositions, those found in religious creeds for example, which can *only* be statements, if they are anything at all? If there are, then it must in their case be a serious matter to be told that they must either be empirically verifiable or meaningless. Thus, even if we bear carefully in mind that the significance of statements alone is in question, the thesis of Logical Positivism can be seen to be no harmless truism. Those who were goaded, during the '20s and '30s, into the excited defence of religion or ethics or aesthetics were really quite right in regarding the verification principle as no laughing matter.

It was probably supposed at one time, though not for very long, that Logical Positivism represented the introduction, at last, into philosophy of principles at once clear, simple, and decisive. It was however not long before complications broke out again. There were, for instance, always some who maintained that the status assigned to sense-experience was unwarranted. It might well be admitted that, if a statement has any definite meaning or content, there must be at any rate some *difference* between the situation in which it would be true, and that, or those, in which it would be false; also that, if so, it must be in principle possible that we should find out which it is; and further, that the process of finding this out must involve having experiences, of some sort or other, the occurrence of which would determine the question. But why, it might be asked, should it be supposed that these experiences must be *sense*-experiences? To make this assumption at once entails that only the most ordinary empirical statements will prove to be meaningful; but why should this assumption be granted? Are there not, or may there not be, experiences, and hence meaningful statements, of sorts quite different from those which the Positivists admitted? In the absence of any satisfactory account of experiences of those supposed other sorts, this objection remained perhaps somewhat theoretical; but it was also difficult to eliminate.

More serious, however, at least at the time, was the fact that, even in the judgement of Positivists themselves, there arose grave internal difficulties in their position. These all arose out of the problem of defining exactly what was to be meant by 'verification'. It seems, for example, reasonable to say that, so far as I am concerned, verifying any statement must consist in my having, now or in the future, experiences of the appropriate sort. But from this two odd consequences seem to follow. First, does it not follow, according to the verification principle, that any statement, even a statement which purports to refer to the past, must *really* mean (so far as I am concerned) something about my present or future experience? If verification can occur only now or in future, can I ever succeed in really *meaning* something about the past? Second, can it really be that any two people ever mean or understand the same thing? Verification for you must occur in your experience, and for me in mine. Hence, what any statement really means must apparently be systematically different for each person who does or might hear or read, speak or write it. How then do we succeed in communicating with each other? What I mean, others can necessarily not understand.

To deal with this difficulty drastic measures were adopted. An attempt was made by some to maintain that this queer 'linguistic solipsism', this apparently ineluctable privacy of meaning, did not matter—that the general intelligibility of language could be saved without denying it. Others adopted the more strenuous policy of asserting that individual reports of sense-experience, though they appeared to be subjective, to be about the private experiences of each reporter, must really be understood as referring in every case to publicly observable, physical events. Thus, the statement 'I feel hot', for example, can be said to mean the same to anyone at all as it does to me, at the expense of maintaining that, even for me, it really refers only to the condition of my body, and not, as it appears to do, to my private feelings. This bold but astonishingly unplausible doctrine was given the appropriate name of 'physicalism', and unfortunately confused, particularly by Neurath, with a quite different thesis about the 'unity of science'.

A still more extraordinary development was this. It is clear that the Logical Positivist thesis was, in origin, an extreme version of empiricism; significant discourse was to be exhibited as firmly tied down to verifiable empirical facts. But in the end this bed-rock itself melted away. For reasons similar to those already mentioned in discussion of Wittgenstein's *Tractatus*, it came to be held that the relation of language to fact could not be a topic of significant discourse. There could be (so-called) statements *of* fact, which were supposed to be the concern of, broadly, scientists; there could also be 'syntactical' statements about the inter-relations of linguistic expressions—these were the philosopher's proper concern. But statements purporting to specify the relation of a linguistic expression *to* fact would belong to neither of these aseptic classes, and hence must be disallowed. If so, the assertion that any statement is verified, that is, found to be true, would have to be understood as asserting a relation *not* between that statement and fact, but between the statement and *other statements*. Thus, we might say, the non-linguistic component simply drops out of the picture, and continued talk of empirical facts must be held to be at best misleading. The Positivists, who in general were nothing if not devoted to their principles, made the best for a time of this position of linguistic imprisonment; but their fellow-travellers and others could hardly resist the suspicion that all was not going as well as had been hoped.

The gradual accumulation of difficulties in maintaining the simple purity of the philosophical doctrine, combined with the physical dissolution of the group as a result of the war, brought about the virtual extinction of Logical Positivism as a coherent movement. Its once canalized energies ran, in some cases, into rather different channels, and in other cases, unfortunately into the sand. Some general assessment of its achievement and character will be attempted in the chapter that follows.

5

First Retrospect

BEFORE PASSING FROM the philosophy of yesterday to that of today we may try the effect of an even more rapid, more Olympian survey of the position now reached, and its relation to a lengthier history. Very general remarks may be helpful, and are not always untrue. It is no doubt perilous to make them. But that cannot be helped.

In the species of Idealism which appeared so suddenly and violently in this country in the later years of the nineteenth century there was, perhaps, nothing fundamentally new. The notion that the proper concern of the philosopher was with the question 'What is the ultimate nature of Reality?' was a notion at least as old as Plato, and arguably older. Moreover it had long been felt, more or less confusedly, that this was no ordinary empirical question; there had been a persistent and quite proper tendency, as more and more aspects and departments of life and the world were made the subjects of systematic empirical study, to distinguish these as not within the philosopher's province. The philosopher's method of inquiry was to consist in reasoning. He was to consider—not challenging, or at least not challenging on their own level, the factual findings of other investigators—how Reality, how things in general, ought to be viewed, in such a way as to satisfy the demands of reason. Of course, what reason demands is not immediately clear; and in fact past philosophers could be quite illuminatingly classified in terms of the startlingly divergent answers they gave, or very often assumed, to the question what these demands were. What determined these answers might be said to be their various senses of what was satisfactory, ideally intelligible. Some found their ideal in tight deductive systems; others, very differently, in the notion of physical mechanism. Others again preferred explanations in terms of purpose. And there were some, as Hume in certain moods but pre-eminently Kant, whose concern was with the question whether *any* view could be both convincingly demonstrable and rationally satisfying.

Absolute Idealism can be distinguished chiefly as being a system for extremists. The supposed satisfactoriness only of the undifferentiated Absolute entailed the consequence that, in order to satisfy reason's demands, the whole apparatus not only of our, but of any, system of thought and speech must be dismantled, and a view substituted which might be occasionally guessed at or glimpsed, but which certainly could never be embodied in sober statement. In natural but perhaps unholy alliance with this novel extremism of thought, there occurred a striking rise in the temperature of philosophical writing. With honourable exceptions, the Idealists brought into British philosophy a species of vivid, violent, and lofty imprecision which even in general literature had hitherto been rare. That this was so was by no means unimportant. It helped them to convey a vague general impression that they were concerned with far deeper questions, and concerned with them far more seriously and intently, than any of their predecessors had ever been. This impression has survived in some quarters to plague their successors. It was doubtless not dishonestly conveyed; but it is certainly mistaken. It is not an indication of blindness or bias to distinguish between the importance of what is said, and the emphasis or eccentricity in the manner of saying it. That distinction is often extremely important in philosophy.

From the point of view of this striking but short-lived philosophical extremism, Moore appears as a far more extraordinary figure than Russell. Certainly, Russell's world of indefinitely numerous, independent logical atoms is the metaphysical opposite of Bradley's Absolute. Certainly, the kind of logic which he thought of as exhibiting the pattern of linguistic perfection, and therefore the true picture of reality, was as far removed as possible from anything that Bradley would have felt to be satisfactory. His respect for mathematics and physics was un-Idealistic. But there is a sense, even so, in which he was playing the same game. He had his own strange notion of the rationally satisfactory, and in terms of it tried to 'give an account' of the world. What was new in this enterprise (and doubtless exceedingly important) was the detail of its execution; its general character was, on the contrary, wholly traditional. Moore, however, was a quite new kind of important philosopher. Though he did not deny the legitimacy of metaphysical ambitions, he was himself entirely without them. If (as he has said himself) his passion for argument had not been provoked into action by the strange doings of others, he might never have been a philosopher at all. For, in general, he did not feel it to be difficult at all to make out a world-view that would satisfy reason's demands. He found the view we all hold, the 'Common Sense view of the world', to be perfectly unsurprising, undistressing, quite certainly true. No doubt he would have regarded as open to discussion the question what exactly does and does not form part of the Common Sense view; perhaps he would have wished to adjust it a little here and there; and, being what he was, this might have occupied him for quite a long time. But this was not what he was really interested in doing. Quite certain of the truth of most things that we ordinarily believe, and profoundly sceptical of the possibility of deciding on the truth or falsehood of large metaphysical theories, he engaged with astonishing pertinacity in the clarification—which he conceived as meaning the *analysis*—of any propositions, philosophical or otherwise, that engaged his interest. He never claimed that this was all that a philosopher could properly do; but this is in fact what, predominantly, he himself did. Part of the great interest and importance of this for others consists, I would suggest, in the fact that this is something which anyone can do—to practise philosophy in the manner of Moore, it is not necessary to have (as most of us doubtless have not) nor to pretend to have (as some at least would be unwilling to do) large-scale metaphysical anxieties. It is necessary only to want to get things clear. And this aim can be pursued, as it was conspicuously by Moore, with an utter absence of pretension, an air of intellectual respectability, provided otherwise by Russell, otherwise again by Cook Wilson and Prichard, but by Idealism at least not always. There are no doubt many who also take satisfaction in the absence from Moore's manner of writing of any aspiration to inappropriate literary virtues. Philosophy as he has pursued it can be seen to be work.

What then are the bearings in this setting of Logical Positivism?

Here the situation is decidedly an odd one, owing, as so often, to discordance between theory and practice. In theory the Positivists had made a most radical departure. For they held, as it had never been held before, that philosophers as such could have no concern at all with questions of fact. The logical analysis of language was not regarded, as it had been by Russell and Moore and in some degree by all earlier philosophers, as *part* of the philosopher's business, but as the whole of it; it was explicitly held that there was nothing else for him to do. Positivists sometimes maintained, in defensive mood, that they ought not to be regarded as revolutionaries—for had not all philosophers from Plato onwards spent much of their time on the niceties of linguistic analysis? Certainly they had. But it had not hitherto been contended that language alone formed the entire subject-matter of philosophy. Those who maintained that this was radically new were quite right, and those who denied it were, perhaps, less than ingenuous.

However, I believe that to a really Olympian eye the Positivists, again, would look less extraordinary than Moore. For in fact they had, surely, their own metaphysical beliefs. Even if their attachment to the Verification Principle is not, as it quite plainly could be, construed as itself expressing a metaphysical conviction, their later doctrines of Physicalism and the 'unity of science' fairly clearly express a particular world-view, a particular ideal of rational acceptability. They were no more reluctant than, say, Bradley would have been to throw over the plain opinions of the plain man, if these could not be squared with the demands of their peculiar principles. No doubt such disagreements were, in their careful moments, represented as not factual, but as 'syntactical' or analytic; but this, even if it were true, would not be decisive; for even the most overtly metaphysical paradox is not quite *ordinarily* at odds with our common opinions.

Continuing our lofty retrospect over the recent past, we may well be struck next by the very curious fact that all the successors of the Idealist empire, however variously related to it by practice or theory, had among themselves a strong family resemblance. Their interests, their principles, and even their prejudices turned out in fact to be remarkably alike. First, they had all arrived by their different routes at the view that the day-to-day labours of the philosopher consisted overwhelmingly in the *analysis of language*. For Moore this was simply the route to clearer understanding, a preliminary perhaps to metaphysical theory, but in practice taking up almost all of his time and attention. For the Logical Atomists the analysis of language was regarded as itself the key to metaphysical truth. Their whole thesis was derived in part, as Russell avowed, from the study of logic conceived as the syntax of a 'perfect language'; and the so-called 'location', through the fog of our imperfect language, of the ultimate facts that we really refer to, was to be achieved by the logical analysis of propositions. The Positivists were also engaged in linguistic analysis, officially without metaphysical ambitions; theirs was supposed to be the two-sided task, on the one hand of exposing the muddles of metaphysicians, and on the other hand of humbly clarifying the vocabularies of the scientist and the mathematician. Thus, in spite of their very substantial divergences in aim and disagreements in doctrine, what each party actually did was very much the same.

But the resemblance in practice went also further than this. All parties were alike, not only in their concern with language, but also in their predominant concern with a particular part of it. They were interested almost exclusively in statements of fact, or at any rate—to bring logic and mathematics into the picture—in truths. This is not, of course, in the least surprising. The Positivists wished to distinguish the truths of science from the alleged truths of metaphysics, and hence were concerned to draw a clear distinction between genuine statements of fact and mere impostors. The Atomists, bent on the location of atomic facts, had of course to take ordinary statements of fact as their point of departure. And Moore was mainly concerned with the analysis of what was, or at least might perhaps be, *true*, and hence he too made statements the topic of his inquiries.

More interesting, perhaps, is the further point that certain prejudices about statements were also common to all parties. This is shown in the commonly accepted notion of 'analysis', and in the commonly held conviction that analysis of this type was entirely adequate for philosophical purposes. The search for philosophical analyses always took the form of an attempt to formulate a sort of linguistic equation. On the left of the equation was to be the expression to be analysed, and on the right another expression, usually longer and more explicit, designed to be synonymous with or equivalent to the first—equivalent in the sense of being entailed by, entailing, and being logically independent of the very same things. It seems not to have been doubted that language did actually have the rather simple and perfectly rigid articulation presupposed by this faith in simple linguistic equations; nor does it appear to have occasioned any discomfort that they leave out of account all questions of non-verbal *context*—questions, that is, about the characteristic situations or circumstances in which, or purposes for which, linguistic expressions are typically employed. The practitioners of analysis operated in effect, implicitly, with a startlingly simplified picture of what a language is—the picture of a firmly and simply articulated system of expressions employed, not indeed without reference to fact, but in other respects in a total contextual vacuum, for the one sole purpose of stating things truly or falsely. The Logical Atomists can be said to have adopted this picture quite deliberately as representing the real state of affairs. For others it was implicit only. But it was certainly present. For unless one pictured language to oneself in this way, it would be unreasonable to attach so much value to the standard procedure of analysis. It would be too clear that analyses of the standard pattern might often be undiscoverable, or if discovered, then often so very thinly informative as scarcely to merit the labour of formulation.

Thus there was in philosophical circles, until the later 1930s, a large measure of uniformity in practice, overlying, and to a great extent concealing from view, considerable diversity in aims and doctrines. It is not surprising that the situation was often then, and has often been since, misunderstood. It has been particularly tempting, I believe, for commentators outside the professional ring to identify, first, what in fact was common to all parties— pre-occupation with analysis of language; next, to take note of the novel idea that this was the sole proper business of philosophy —an idea sponsored only by Logical Positivism; and finally, confusing this singularity of doctrine with the general uniformity of practice, to decide that all philosophers of the day were Logical Positivists. This was in fact not true at any time. I am inclined to think that it was not even true that those philosophers who really were Logical Positivists were the most revolutionary or radical figures. By profession they were. But by temperament, by practice, and by force of example, far more difference was made, I believe, by the work of Moore. He was not only among the first to oppose both the manner and the matter of the Idealist 'tradition'; he was also far more profoundly unlike its practitioners. By comparison the Logical Atomists and even the Positivists have very much of the look of traditional figures. Their work has a truly 'philosophical' air which would not have been quite strange, though it might well have seemed disagreeable, to their predecessors. Moore's work is in essence so simple, so direct, so wholly unprejudiced and candid, as scarcely to seem philosophical at all. It is just argument. That, perhaps, is its peculiar virtue, and the secret of its power.

6
Wittgenstein

---

1. Language

THERE CAN BE NO serious doubt that the most powerful and pervasive influence upon the practice of philosophy in this country today has been that of Ludwig Wittgenstein. An account of his work and its effect presents peculiar difficulties; but an attempt to provide one, provisional no doubt and very imperfect, must be made.

The causes of difficulty at this point are various. In the first place, chronology becomes somewhat confusing. Wittgenstein's *Tractatus* was published in 1921, and in English translation in the following year. For a few years thereafter he lived near Vienna, being at that time in fairly close touch with, though never one of, the philosophers of the Vienna Circle; and he had been in England from 1912 to 1914, spending part of that period in Cambridge as a pupil of Russell's. He returned to Cambridge in 1929, and from about that date onwards his philosophical work began to take on a radically different character. However, for one reason or another, it was several years before anything much was generally known of these new developments. Not only did Wittgenstein publish nothing himself; he seems also to have been strongly opposed to any publication by those to whom his ideas were imparted. Several years passed before even articles bearing the new character were generally available, and even these were, to say the least, unauthorized by Wittgenstein himself. At the same time interest in his work was so strong in many quarters that reports of it did in fact achieve a considerable though half-clandestine currency. These could not be regarded, of course, as final or authoritative; but by 1953, when his *Philosophical Investigations*[1] were posthumously published, a good many philosophers had been for several years more or less familiar with the trend of his work. It is thus difficult or even impossible to say just when or how his influence, after 1929, began to operate. It was certainly widely diffused well before 1953, but the peculiar circumstances of its diffusion baffle exact historical description.

The description of his work itself is also peculiarly difficult. The *Philosophical Investigations* do not even look like most earlier or later philosophical writing, and almost certainly suffer far more damage from being put into a nut-shell. The book consists of a succession of brief, often loosely connected paragraphs; as Wittgenstein says, it travels 'over a wide field of thought crisscross in every direction'; it is full of unanswered questions, unamplified hints, imaginary dialogues, images, metaphors, and epigrams. One may well wonder how this impassioned notebook is related to the orderly, decorous, argumentative treatises of other earlier and later philosophers. Does it really belong to the same subject at all? The fact is, of course, that it does; but it is not at all easy to relate what is found in its pages to what goes on elsewhere. Wittgenstein, in fact, would not much have wanted to do this. He was comparatively uninterested in the doings of other philosophers, whether of the past or of his own time. For the most part it was with himself that he argued most vehemently.

Fundamental to the change in his philosophical views which occurred quite soon after his *Tractatus* was published was a radically altered conception of language. In order to see what this change was, we must consider very briefly the position from which he began. This was in fact closely related to Russell's Logical Atomism; it could be called perhaps a more consistent, more thorough, and therefore more extreme working out of some of Russell's principles and ideas. Wittgenstein in a sense took these ideas more seriously; he saw more deeply into their consequences. We have already mentioned his startling realization that, if what he himself had written was true, then it must for the most part also be meaningless; and we have seen that he did not shrink

[1] Blackwell, 1953. German text and English translation by G. E. M. Anscombe. The paragraphs are numbered, and in what follows are referred to by numbers alone.

from avowing this. He also paid more attention than Russell had done to the ways in which language must be supposed to be related to the world of which we wish to speak, and to the character of the 'logical atoms' of which, according to the doctrine, reality was composed. On both points his views were ruthlessly peculiar.

Like Russell, he located the real link between language and reality in the relation of atomic propositions to atomic facts. His general conception of this relation is well suggested in his own comparison with *pictures*. In a picture of an object or scene, there is a kind of correspondence between the parts of or elements in the picture, and the parts of or elements in the object or scene. But these elements must not only be present; their structure, form, or arrangement must be the same—according of course to some system of projection, whether simple perspective or something more elaborate. Now 'an atomic fact is a combination of objects (entities, things). . . . The configuration of objects forms the atomic fact.'[1] But the 'sentential sign' is itself also a fact; it too is a combination of elements, namely *words*. This sort of fact is therefore capable of 'picturing' those other, non-verbal facts; and it is thus that language can refer to the world, can *mean* something other than itself. What were the elements of these facts taken to be? On the side of language they were said to be, in a queer sense, names, simple demonstrative symbols; on the side of reality they were objects, 'particulars'. But a particular cannot be, as Russell had supposed, such a thing as a white dot or a red patch. For that a particular is white or red is merely a fact about it; it *itself* is merely what *can* be white or red, and can be said (misleadingly perhaps) to be really colourless.[2] And since an object is what *can* enter into a 'configuration', it must not itself *be* a configuration; it must be simple.

But not all propositions of any actual language are atomic propositions, pictures of atomic facts. So what are the propositions that we actually utter? Here, as we have seen, the thorough-going answer was ready to hand; they are truth-functional compounds of atomic propositions. Atomic propositions are, as it were, the nearly-undetectable bricks out of which our daily utterances are built; and the rules of construction, hard though it may be to see

[1] *Tractatus*, 2.01, 2.0272.
[2] ibid. 2.032.

that is so, are (more or less) the rules of combination laid down in *Principia Mathematica*. No doubt we often utter sets of words which are not thus constructed; sometimes we do this through sheer confusion, sometimes (as perhaps in expressing ethical judgements) we do it for more serious purposes; but in all such cases it has to be concluded that we do not really *say* anything— our words have no *meaning*, for meaning is derivable alone, in certain ways alone, from atomic propositions.

Now it was, of course, always clear that this account of language was not any sort of empirical description; it was not based on observation. If one were asked simply to observe a language and describe it, one's account would certainly be utterly unlike this. Indeed it was a point constantly stressed that language does *not* appear to fit with this account, that one's natural impressions of it are utterly different. What this account was intended to be was an exposition of the *essence* of language; an account of its concealed foundations; an excavation, so to speak, to its deepest level. The attempt was to bring into the light what language conceals —its own hidden workings, its essential bones that are normally unseen beneath the familiar surface. The account offered was thus in no way *seen* to be a true one; it was maintained only that, if we think about the essence of language and neglect its merely superficial features, we shall see that the foundations *must* be as thus described.

It appears that within the space of a few years after 1921 Wittgenstein came to believe that this queer, non-empirical account of language was not, as it claimed to be, the exposure of something deeply concealed, but on the contrary was the foisting of an invention upon the facts. He came to reject in particular three of the implications or assumptions of his earlier views—first, that language is essentially used for *one* purpose, the stating of facts; second, that sentences essentially get their meanings in *one* way, namely through 'picturing'; and third, that any language essentially has, though it may be hard to see it, the clear and firm structure of the formulae in a logical calculus.

Suppose, he now says that we make a serious attempt to 'command a clear view of the aim and functioning of words'. The first essential point is to observe how various in fact these are. 'Think of the tools in a tool-box; there is a hammer, pliers, a saw, a screwdriver, a rule, a glue-pot, glue, nails and screws. The

functions of words are as diverse as the functions of these objects.'[1]
We may be tempted, especially when we are doing philosophy, to
offer *one* account of the way words function; but any such single
account is, at best, quite useless—as useless as would be, for
example, some *one* account of what tools are for. What would be
gained by saying, for example, 'All tools serve to modify something'? This really tells us nothing at all about tools. It is not
even much use to say that there are many kinds of tools; for how
many 'kinds' are there? 'How many kinds of sentence are there?
Say assertion, question, and command?—There are *countless*
kinds: countless different kinds of use of what we call "symbols",
"words", "sentences". And this multiplicity is not something
fixed.'[2] Words are used in giving orders, describing things, expressing wishes; in play-acting, translating, telling stories; in asking, thanking, cursing, greeting, praying. . . . 'It is interesting to
compare the multiplicity of the tools in language and of the ways
they are used, the multiplicity of kinds of word and sentence,
with what logicians have said about the structure of language.
(Including the author of the *Tractatus Logico-Philosophicus*.)'[3]

Suppose now that someone were to object that all these differences in uses of words were merely surface phenomena, that there
must be some *essential* use of language concealed beneath them—
as indeed Wittgenstein himself once supposed that there was. We
can then ask, why *must* there be one essential use? Is it supposed
that, because they are all called 'uses of language', they must have
something in common? If so, consider the case of *games*. 'What is
common to them all?—Don't say: "There *must* be something
common, or they would not be called 'games'"—but *look and
see* whether there is anything common at all. For if you look at
them you will not see something that is common to *all*, but
similarities, relationships, and a whole series of them at that. To
repeat: don't think, but look!'[4] To suppose that something *must*
be the case, instead of looking to see whether it *is* the case, is one
of the many short roads to philosophical entanglement.

In short, 'the more narrowly we examine actual language, the
sharper becomes the conflict between it and our requirement.'[5]
We are constantly struck by more and more variety in the actual
or possible uses of words, and borne further and further away

[1] 11. [2] 23. [3] ibid. [4] 66. [5] 107.

from the idea that language ('as such' perhaps) has just one use. In order to bring out the full scope of this variety, Wittgenstein not only points out various uses in existing language, but also imagines possible languages, simplified in such a way as to bring their multifold variety clearly into view.

Consider next the related idea that words get their meanings in some one way. Perhaps 'one thinks that learning language consists in giving names to objects'.[1] But there are enormously many words that could not be thought to be names of anything. Besides, what is 'giving a name' to something? Perhaps pointing at it and uttering the name. But of course, if this is to be successful, the performance must be understood in the proper way; there are always many different ways in which it *could* be understood. If you point to something and say 'That is oval', I shall thereby learn what 'oval' means only if I already understand that you are referring to its shape. And how does this differ from referring to its colour, or to the object itself? 'How he "takes" the definition is seen in the use that he makes of the word defined'—and since there are very many different uses even of common nouns and adjectives, it is clear that learning by the supposedly single process of being 'given the name' must really be no less various. Even naming has to be understood in as many ways as there are uses of names. 'What is the relation between name and thing named?— Well, what *is* it?'[2]—we have to look at particular cases, and *find out* what is involved in coming to understand words, learning what they mean; and we shall find that very many quite different things are involved.

Consider next the *structure* of language. Is it the case that the propositions we ordinarily utter are complex, built up in accordance with precise rules of construction from exactly specifiable simpler elements? Is it true that there must be certain exact logical relations between the quite diverse things that we say? Well, why should one suppose that this *must* be true? 'F. P. Ramsey once emphasized in conversation with me that logic was a "normative science". I do not know exactly what he had in mind, but it was doubtless closely related to what only dawned on me later: namely, that in philosophy we often *compare* the use of words with games and caculi which have fixed rules, but cannot say that someone who is using language *must* be playing such a game.'[1] It is even dangerous to say that a language embodying fixed and clear rules would be an 'ideal' language. For 'the most that can be said is that we *construct* ideal languages'; these are not, as for instance Russell had implied, better or more 'perfect' than our ordinary language—'as if it took the logician to show people at last what a correct sentence looked like'. 'We misunderstand the role of the ideal in our language. . . . The idea now absorbs us, that the ideal *"must"* be found in reality. Meanwhile we do not as yet see *how* it occurs there, nor do we understand the nature of this "must". We think it must be in reality; for we think we already see it there.' Though the most obvious phenomena of language seem to conflict with this belief in a fixed, simple, and definite structure, 'the strict and clear rules of the logical structure of propositions appear to us as something in the background—hidden in the medium of the understanding'. But 'where does this idea come from? It is like a pair of glasses on our nose through which we see whatever we look at. It never occurs to us to take them off.'[2]

But suppose that we do take them off and look again at the facts. 'The more narrowly we examine actual language, the sharper becomes the conflict between it and our requirement. . . . We see that what we call "sentence" and "language" have not the formal unity that I imagined, but are families of structures more or less related to one another.' The idea of an underlying 'crystalline purity' was not a result of investigation; it was a *preconceived idea*. The 'perfect language' of Logical Atomism was not a discovery, something uncovered beneath the confusing wrappings of ordinary language—it was something invented, which gave to its inventors the illusion that they had found it, could somehow see it to be hiding *behind* what they well knew to be apparently so different. But were they right in supposing this difference to be only apparent? With our spectacles off, we can see no reason to think so.

So far, then, what Wittgenstein has to say amounts simply to this: that language *is not*—not even 'essentially' or in some covert way—as he himself and others had once represented it. There is no one pattern to be revealed, no single account to be offered, no

[1] 81.　　　　　　　　[2] 100-3.

small set of definite rules. On the contrary, the forms and uses of
language are inexhaustibly flexible and various; a language is
not like *a* game, but like a whole family of games, and the rules
for, the purposes of, the ways of playing these games are themselves endlessly diverse. To this we must add one rather different
point, to which Wittgenstein alludes only briefly and occasionally.
We must, he says, resist the temptation to think of language as
something unique, something isolated and quite on its own; we
must not make it appear to ourselves as something *strange*. Using
a language is not only *among* the most ordinary things that we do
—'as much a part of our natural history as walking, eating, drink-
ing, playing';[1] it is also in countless ways actually involved in
many other things that we do, so that it without them is unintelligible, and they without it. 'To imagine a language means to
imagine a form of life'[2]—so that often the explanation, or the
understanding, of language must bring in what at first sight
looks wholly non-linguistic, something, simply, about what people
are, and want, and do.

2. *Logical Atomism*

But now, of course, we have something that needs explanation.
Suppose it to be agreed, as I imagine it would be, that Wittgenstein's new way of looking at language, even in the rough description that we have just given, is reasonable, realistic, clear-sighted,
illuminating; and that by comparison the *Tractatus* account, however powerful and impressive in its way, does really look like a
myth, a theorist's fantasy. Suppose it to be agreed also, as it
manifestly should be, that Wittgenstein and Russell were not less,
but far more, perceptive and penetrating than most of us are. How
then could it possibly have come about that they accepted this
fantasy, with positive fervour, as if it were a fundamental truth?

It is remarkable that, in his *Investigations*, Wittgenstein did
not deploy any set, systematic attack on his own earlier views; he
did not attempt to say just what mistakes were made, what bad
arguments used, what distinctions missed. Now his refusal to
proceed in this way, though it might seem to add to his readers'
difficulties, was deliberate. For he believed that what lay behind
the old way of thinking was not a mistake of fact or logic, nor

[1] 25.   [2] 19.

even a cluster of such mistakes, but something better called a
superstition. And how is one to deal with a superstitious man?
Suppose he believes that natural events are the work of demons.
It would not help him to say, for example, 'But look, it is only
the match that makes the paper catch fire; it really isn't true that
there is a demon at work'—for until one has somehow shaken or
removed his entire system of queer ideas, he can only see the
phenomena you show him in the light of them, still as the work
of demons. What we need is not to point out this mistake or that,
but 'to turn our whole examination round'.[1] It is not, to put the
point rather differently, that Russell and Wittgenstein were not
intelligent enough to detect mistakes and flaws in their reasoning;
it was as if their intelligence was 'bewitched'; they did not simply
overlook the true facts of the case, but in some way were *unable*
to see those facts in the natural way. We have, then, not to detect
mistakes, but to dethrone a superstition, defeat a bewitchment;
it is the *source* of the trouble that is to be exposed, not the errors
which were simply its natural manifestations.

. What then was the source, or were the sources, of the superstition? Here we find a curious position. The source of the superstitious beliefs about language is, as Wittgenstein argues, language
itself. We have to resist 'the bewitchment of our intelligence
by means of language', superstitions 'produced by grammatical
illusions', 'through a misinterpretation of our forms of language';[2] therefore, we must look 'into the workings of our
language, and that in such a way as to make us recognize those
workings: *in despite of* an urge to misunderstand them'. We
must make it our aim to 'command a clear view', in spite of the
fact that 'our forms of expression prevent us in all sorts of ways'
from seeing clearly what lies before us.

What is meant by 'the bewitchment of our intelligence by
means of language'? Something like this: there are in our language certain forms of question, for example, which suggest—perhaps
because most questions of that form would receive—a certain form
of answer; or there are, in general, forms of expression which
suggest—perhaps because they often have—a certain kind of interpretation. Yet, in some cases, it may be that the form of answer
which a question suggests is not really appropriate to just that
question; or that, more generally, a certain expression cannot

[1] 108.   [2] 109, 110.

rightly be interpreted in the kind of way that its form seems to require. But it may be extremely difficult, and particularly so in the practice of philosophy, to recognize such cases for what they are; we may be unable to resist the suggestion of our forms of language, and hence persist in the attempt to find answers to questions, or to interpret expressions, in ways that are quite inappropriate to the cases at issue. It is, one might say, as if the surface of our language were thickly covered with well-trodden paths, and we were constantly tempted to follow these paths even when they did not lead in the direction we were trying to go.

Consider, for example, what became in the hands of the Atomists of the question 'What is a name?' What came to mind first, it seems, was a certain simple procedure of naming—the object is before us and we give it its name, as Adam did with the animals. But to be named in this way an object must both exist and be presented to the namer. But can I not say, of a ship that has been blown up and of which the pieces are at the bottom of the sea, 'The *Britannia* struck a mine and sank'? And in saying this do I not use the name of an object not present, which indeed no longer exists? Russell's answer would have been that 'Britannia' is not a real name; no doubt I can *describe* what is absent or no longer exists, but I cannot (as Adam did with the animals) *name* it; so 'Britannia' must really be a description in disguise, and so indeed must be everything we commonly think of as a name. 'The whole business of proper names,' Russell said, 'is rather curious'—so curious indeed that he came to the conclusion that 'the only words one does use as names in the logical sense are words like "this" or "that" ',[1] words certainly which it would never enter one's head, in the ordinary way, to classify as names.

But what was it that led him into this curious view? What indeed made Wittgenstein at one time inclined to agree with him? In this case, as in others, 'a *picture* held us captive'[2]—the simple picture of names as assigned by Adam to the animals, as thus confined to the case of what exists and is present before us. This picture is, undoubtedly, a picture of naming—'and we could not get outside it, for it lay in our language and language seemed to repeat it to us inexorably'. It is true that the actual uses of actual names are in most cases nothing like that which the picture suggested. But two forces combined to push that fact into

[1] *Logic and Knowledge*, p. 201.   [2] 115.

the background. First—and this was another case of 'grammatical illusion'—the fact that the question 'What is a name?' seemed difficult to answer was assumed to be due to the fact that the answer was somehow *hidden*—that the *real* nature of names was in some way concealed *behind* the plain facts as to actual uses of names, so that these actual uses should be kept out of the way, should not be looked *at* but rather seen *through*. Second, in the course of the philosophical discussion names were considered without a context, not in use, but as if taken out of use for more careful inspection. But words out of use are apt to get out of control. Thus 'naming appears as a *queer* connection of a word with an object.—And you really get such a queer connection when the philosopher tries to bring out *the* relation between name and thing by staring at an object in front of him and repeating a name or even the word "this" innumerable times. . . . And we can also say the word "this" *to* the object, as it were *address* the object as "this"—a queer use of this word, which doubtless only occurs in doing philosophy.'[1] Words thus inspected, repeated, thought about in abstraction from any actual use are liable to pose as having most peculiar uses which perhaps none actually has 'in the language-game which is its original home'. The harder one thinks in such a contextless vacuum, the more hopelessly 'bewitched' one is liable to become; 'one thinks that one is tracing the outline of the thing's nature over and over again, and one is merely tracing round the frame through which we look at it.'[2]

More generally: the Atomists had been ostensibly concerned with such questions as 'What is a language? How do sentences *mean* something? What is a name, and what sort of things can be named?' The answers to these questions were not obvious; and here the first 'picture' began to operate. If the answers were not obvious, then obvious phenomena surely could not be relevant to the problem; the answer must surely be something quite different, something which the things we all see merely conceal. What then? And here countless other pictures, 'preconceived ideas', came into play—the picture of a calculus with clear and fixed rules, the picture of naming, the picture of dismantling something composite in order to discover its basic components, the picture indeed of a picture and what it portrays. All these and many others combined to produce the conviction that language *must* be,

[1] 38.   [2] 114.

could *only* be, like this or like that—and at the same time to keep out of sight the actual facts, too obvious to be noticed or to seem important. All these pictures, so Wittgenstein suggests, are embodied in the forms of language itself. It is language itself which works to prevent the realization of its own character. To see how this is so is to have defeated the superstition. It is comparable rather with conversion than with the detection of error.

3. *Philosophical Problems*

So far, we have sketched the way in which Wittgenstein came to see the problems of Logical Atomism. These problems he explained as due primarily to an attempt to impose upon language a 'preconceived', artificial view which was, when once one came to look at language with open eyes, startlingly inadequate to its actual variousness, complexity, flexibility; and the urge to make this attempt he attributed to an 'illusion', a superstition arising in some way out of language itself. From this point he came, even jumped, to the bold conclusion that *all* philosophical problems are of this type.

This conclusion was certainly not reached by induction. At no time, I believe, did Wittgenstein make any wide historical survey of philosophy in order to test his opinion against actual evidence. He believed no doubt that it was in fact true of his own problems, those with which he had himself been engaged in his earlier years. He perhaps thought also that his view *must* be true, if there were to be a distinct class of 'philosophical' problems at all. And perhaps he was also half-unconsciously inclined to make his view generally true by definition—that is, to classify a problem as philosophical only if it could be interpreted in the light of his views. Let us consider again, more generally, what those views were.

First, then, what is a philosophical problem like? Or what sort of problem is it to which we are inclined to give the name 'philosophical'? In Wittgenstein's view what marks off such a problem is a characteristic *unclarity*, a certain power to baffle and confuse. 'A philosophical problem has the form: "I don't know my way about".'[1] This sort of problem arises typically in cases where certainly it is not ignorance that defeats us. What is more thoroughly

[1] 123.

familiar to us, for example, than perception, the use of our senses? Yet here there has repeatedly arisen a most formidable cluster of baffling problems. Conversely, if it *is* ignorance that defeats us, we do not feel ourselves to be faced by a philosophical problem. Questions about the structure of the remoter galaxies, the causes of cancer, the properties of the human nervous system, are questions to which perhaps we do not know the answers; but we see pretty well what sorts of questions they are, more or less how their answers are to be looked for, and whose specialized business it is to look for those answers. Nor do we feel that a philosophical problem arises where a question is clearly to be answered by some sort of calculation—we see it as a question in mathematics, for instance, or in logic, not in philosophy. A philosophical problem typically gives us the impression that, although we know all that might be relevant to it, yet we cannot see clearly; it is as if we were lost and did not know which way to turn; or as if we had become entangled and could not see how to extricate ourselves. We see all the pieces of the puzzle, but not how they fit together to form a picture. Very often, this shows itself in the baffling fact that the only answer to our question which seems to us possible is also an answer which we cannot believe to be true—'But *this* isn't how it is!'—we say. 'Yet *this* is how it has to be!'[1] It is not that we do not know what is the case, but that we also seem to be driven to deny it.

In Wittgenstein's account of the ways in which such typical predicaments arise two elements can be roughly distinguished. There is, first of all, the plain but extremely important fact that the verbal, surface-grammatical forms of our language are incomparably less various than are the actual uses of words. Such grammatical categories as *noun, adjective, verb,* are no doubt not absolutely straightforward—no doubt one could think of marginal cases that would present difficulties even of grammatical classification; but still, it is clear in the vast majority of cases how words should be grammatically classified, how sentences should be parsed; and the complexity required for these purposes is not overwhelmingly great. But the ways in which words are actually used are enormously more diverse and complex than this. 'Pink', 'past', 'ambitious', are all adjectives; 'believe', 'walk', 'see', are all verbs; 'consciousness', 'table', 'cause' are all nouns. But cutting

[1] 112.

across these gross grammatical resemblances it is clear that there
are immense divergences of use. But it is not, of course, clear at a
glance what these divergences are; 'our grammar is lacking in this
sort of perspicuity';[1] and therefore it is always possible that the
very visible, surface-grammatical resemblances will lead us to
think that there are other resemblances, and even prevent us from
noticing that there are not.

It should not be supposed that this possible way of being misled is surely too simple and obvious to be a philosophical danger.
It would be possible to illustrate its workings in many hundreds
of actual cases. But let us take one to serve as a specimen. Moore,
in examining the old Idealist contention that time is not real,
was once led to raise the question, what the word 'real' means.
But he considers this question in a very peculiar way. We apply
the word 'real' to many things, to things of all kinds—we speak
of a real (as opposed to an illusory) advantage, of a real (as
opposed to a false) beard, of a real (as opposed to a toy) pistol, of
real (as opposed to hallucinatory) pink rats; we employ the word,
that is, to exclude a wide variety of oddities, defects, or deviations,
it being as a rule quite clear from the context what exactly we
mean to exclude in a particular case.[2] Moore, however, raises his
question in this way: what *property* is it that we mean to assert
that all those things which we call 'real' have in common? Now
there is, fairly clearly, no such property at all. When I say that
the juvenile delinquent had a real pistol in his pocket, and that
a long spell in a reformatory would be of real benefit to him, I
do not in the least mean to assert that the benefit and his pistol
have a property in common; but rather to make clear that the
pistol was not a toy, and that the benefit would not be neglig-
ible. Why then did Moore assume, as the form of his question
shows that he did, that there *must* be *one* property of 'reality'?
Was it not because he thought of the *typical adjective* as being
used to ascribe a property common to all those things to which
it applies, and assumed that the word 'real' must be used in this
way because it too is grammatically an adjective? That is, the
very visible adjectival grammar of the word produced an 'illusion'
as to its actual use. Moore in fact fell victim to a similar but
more notorious illusion in his discussion of 'good' in *Principia*

---

[1] 122.
[2] cf. J. L. Austin, *Sense and Sensibilia*, pp. 62–77.

Ethica; this word too, he thought, must connote an 'indefinable' *quality*.

Rather different from but closely connected with this first point is our liability to be swayed, or even 'enslaved', by what Wittgenstein often calls 'pictures', or what could also be called *models* or *standard cases*. In a sense this point includes the first, since it may sometimes occur that a grammatical resemblance induces us to try to assimilate the use of a word to that of some other word of the same grammatical type, which we think of as exhibiting *the*, or the *standard*, use of words of that type. But the issues involved here may go far beyond grammar. Consider, as a simplified example, the notion of *proof*. Now there are proofs of many sorts— geometric proofs, scientific proofs, police-court proofs, proofs of the pudding in the eating, and many others. But it may be that a philosopher becomes obsessed with *one* kind of proof, a particular 'picture' or model or standard of what it is to prove something; and so long as this picture retains its exclusive hold, he may feel obliged to maintain in the teeth of paradox that nothing else is really a proof at all, perhaps even that we do not really *know* anything but what can be proved in his ideal or standard way. Or it may be simply that he feels perplexed by proofs of any other sort—they may seem to him, however familiar, to be puzzling, because they do not fit in with his picture of a proof. There is, Wittgenstein thought, a characteristic way in which such puzzlement as this may arise and then become chronic: there is a certain temptation to suppose that such a question as 'What is a proof?' is a question to be answered just by *thinking*, as it were by inwardly surveying the idea of a proof—by attempting to discern, as Moore often put it, 'what comes before our minds', when we say 'a *proof*'. It is against this notion that Wittgenstein directs the injunction 'Don't think, but look!' For 'does the whole *use* of the word come before my mind, when I *understand* it in this way?'[1] No—the same picture, whatever it may be, simply presents itself over and over again; I repeatedly 'trace round the frame through which I look at it'; constantly seem to confirm my preconceived idea; and never think of *looking to see* what in fact proofs are, how many kinds of procedures are all called 'proofs', and how familiar really these various procedures are.

What then is the remedy for this predicament? The actual

[1] 139.

uses of the word must be identified and described. It is not, of
course, that we do not know what the word in question means; no
doubt we are well able to use it correctly. But we do not 'command a clear view' of its use. It is not that there is anything
obscure or hidden to be discovered; what we need already 'lies
open to view' in the actual uses we make of the word. So we need
to describe these, in order to remind ourselves of them—'the
work of the philosopher consists in assembling reminders for a
particular purpose'.[1] And the purpose here is not only to make
clear the use of the word, but also to oppose the powerful temp-
tations that there may be to misrepresent it. It is true that there
is nothing to be revealed, discovered, or explained—'we must do
away with all *explanation,* and description alone must take its
place.'[2] But this description must not be haphazard and un-
directed; it 'gets its light—i.e. its purpose—from the philosophical
problems. These are, of course, not empirical problems; they are
solved, rather, by looking into the workings of our language, and
that in such a way as to make us recognize those workings: *in
despite of* an urge to misunderstand them. The problems are
solved, not by giving new information, but by arranging what we
have always known. Philosophy is a battle against the bewitchment of our intelligence by means of language.'

4. Philosophical Paradox

Part of the explanation of the notoriety of the Logical Positivists lay, as was mentioned earlier, in their highly polemical and
even abusive characterization of the efforts of very many other
philosophers—in their zeal to attach the label 'meaningless' to
many venerable doctrines, theses, and counter-theses. Now in a
good many passages Wittgenstein says things which would quite
naturally give the impression that he too took this view. It is
worth inquiring how far he actually did so.

Certainly one does get the impression that, according to Wittgenstein, the philosopher's task today is to dispel confusion. 'What
we do is to bring words back from their metaphysical to their
everyday usage'[3]—and to do this, it seems, is to substitute sense
for nonsense. Indeed he does actually say that 'the results of

---

[1] 127.   [2] 109.   [3] 116.

philosophy are the uncovering of one or another piece of plain nonsense';[1] this may seem purely and painfully destructive, but 'what we are destroying is nothing but houses of cards and we are clearing up the ground of language on which they stand'.[2] Again, 'when we do philosophy [i.e. when it is done in the old, unenlightened way], we are like savages, primitive people, who hear the expressions of civilized men, put a false interpretation on them, and then draw the queerest conclusions from it'.[3] He asks himself 'What is your aim in philosophy?'; and he answers 'To show the fly the way out of the fly-bottle'.[4] And where is he when he has made his escape? He is, it appears, exactly where he started; for philosophy 'leaves everything as it is'.[5]

I believe that, in fact, these and a few other passages tend to misrepresent Wittgenstein's real position. He did not really believe that philosophical doctrines were *plain* nonsense, *nothing but* houses of cards, that a philosopher was *merely* a fly in a fly-bottle. Why then did he say these things? They are, in the first place, here detached from their context—they do not stand in his book absolutely unqualified. Moreover they have, like so much of his writing, the character of aphorisms; and the aphorist is not required to go to the stake for the literal, unqualified truth of everything he says. It should also always be remembered that the philosophical 'illusions' which concerned Wittgenstein most deeply and constantly were those to which he had himself been at one time subject; and it is natural to repudiate one's own illusions with a vehemence and even rudeness that one would probably withhold from the illusions of others. When Wittgenstein thought of philosophy in the old style, he tended always to think first of philosophy in his old style; and certainly much of his more sweeping condemnation is primarily addressed to himself.

If for these reasons the remarks quoted above ought to be in some way discounted, how exactly ought they to be qualified or explained? In two ways, I think, both fairly obvious. In the first place, though Wittgenstein speaks of philosophical doctrines as 'houses of cards', he does not think of the business of constructing them as in any way silly or trivial. No doubt very many of the sayings of philosophers really are 'plain nonsense', no more and no less; no doubt they are sometimes the outcome of sheer confusion and nothing else. But these are merely the uninteresting

[1] 119.   [2] 118.   [3] 194.   [4] 309.   [5] 124.

cases. The interesting ones, although they too find expression in queer and distorted uses of language, 'have the character of *depth*. They are deep disquietudes; their roots are as deep in us as the forms of our language and their significance is as great as the importance of our language.'[1] If there is a prejudice which, arising from some pervasive feature of our thought or language, from some 'picture' which our way of speaking imposes upon us, prevents us from recognizing the actual 'workings of our language', this 'is not a *stupid* prejudice'. Its source may lie so deep in our way of thinking that both it, and its removal, may be of the greatest importance to us; for of course the removal of a prejudice must be an affair of no less significance than was the prejudice itself. It may even be that some philosophical tangles are due to 'bumps that the understanding has got by running its head up against the limits of language'[2]—and this makes us at least see where those limits lie. It is true that the ordered description of the workings of language gets its importance only 'from the problems'; but the importance it thus gets is as great as that of the problems themselves. In the end they are simply removed, cleared away; but that they existed was never a trivial matter. They had after all the power to 'bewitch our intelligence'. Should psychiatric treatment of the mentally ill be regarded as trivial on the ground that it leaves a man nothing more exciting than sane?

The second point can be conveniently made with the help of some words of Wittgenstein's own. A philosophical problem, he said, has the form: 'I don't know my way about.' If so, then its successful treatment may indeed 'leave everything as it is', in the sense that it leaves me still in the same place. But it has not made no difference either; for now I *do* know my way about. The point that Wittgenstein had in mind was that it was not the business of philosophy to add to our information, nor yet to alter our language; it makes no difference of this sort. But it does make a difference in that by it we may achieve a clear view, a grasp, a command of what was indeed always there to be seen, but had not before been seen in all its bearings and connections. We *leave* things as they are; but perhaps for the first time we come to *see* them as they are. That this is not a wholly negative result is perhaps clearer in some of Wittgenstein's writings other than the *Investigations*: for example, his *Remarks on the Foundation*

[1] 111.   [2] 119.

of Mathematics, while doubtless they make no change in mathematics, could scarcely fail to show the reader things *about* mathematics that he had not seen before.

Is it necessary here to add that Wittgenstein of course does not suggest that philosophical problems are all 'about language'? Of course they are not; they are about knowledge, memory, truth, space and time, perception, and innumerable other things. What he suggests is that, though thus not *about* language, they typically spring *from* language; they show themselves in distorted uses of language; they reveal confusion as to the uses of language; they are to be solved (or removed) by our coming to see and to employ our language properly. It would make no difference of substance here if one referred, instead of to 'language', to 'concepts'. This may sound more important; but then it was never suggested that the problems were trivial.

Even so, it would be urged by some even of those who accept much of Wittgenstein's theory and practice that the general impression which he gives of philosophy, at least in the *Investigations*, is excessively negative. This has sometimes been urged, for instance, by Professor Wisdom.[1]

Suppose—to take an example which is, as short examples must be, a caricature—that a philosopher asserts that no empirical proposition can be known with certainty to be true. One might respond to this assertion in several ways. Moore for example, with justice, would have been much concerned with the fact that this assertion is obviously false. The proposition that, for instance, some cats are black is certainly an empirical proposition; and of course we all do know with certainty that it is true. So absurd indeed would it be to deny that this and thousands of other similar propositions are known with certainty to be true, that surely the philosopher who denies this must be saying something which he himself knows to be false. How curious it is, but apparently how common, that philosophers should behave in this singular way!

Now Wittgenstein, unlike Moore, would not have been surprised by the fact that the philosopher asserts what is obviously false; for he would have seen this as a characteristic symptom of a philosophical assertion, a signal that the assertor has 'lost his

[1] See, for example, 'Philosophical Perplexity', in *Philosophy and Psychoanalysis* (1953).

way' somewhere in the intricacies of language. His concern would have been directed to the question *why* the philosopher should make—should feel himself compelled to make—an assertion so extraordinary. For of course we do all know, as Moore maintains, that vast numbers of empirical propositions are certainly true. The philosopher cannot simply have failed to notice this; he must have been led into his assertion in spite of it; that is, he was bewitched. What is it then that has bewitched him? Let us suppose that he argued thus: If anything is to be known with certainty to be so, its contradictory must be known to be impossible; but all that we can know to be *impossible* is what we can prove to be self-contradictory; but the contradictory of an empirical proposition, being itself empirical, cannot be self-contradictory; therefore it cannot be known to be impossible; and therefore no empirical proposition can be known with certainty to be true. Now what does this argument do? In effect it identifies what can be *known* with what can be *proved*, and further identifies what can be proved with what can be formally *demonstrated*. Alternatively, or additionally, it appears to identify 'what might (as a matter of fact) be the case', with 'what could (as a matter of logic) be the case', or to make logic the only arbiter of possibility. It seems to embody, that is, a 'picture' of knowledge derived from the fields of mathematics or logic; and so obsessed has the philosopher apparently become with this picture that it has completely distorted his vision. It is as if it had driven him to forget how the words 'know' and 'certainty' actually work—to forget how many cases there actually are in which empirical propositions are, and rightly, said to be known with certainty to be true. Our task, then, must surely be to dispel his confusion by recalling his attention to the actual facts—by confronting his obsessive, exclusive picture of knowledge with all the facts that that picture does not allow for.

Of this sort of corrective procedure Wisdom has complained that it represents philosophical paradoxes 'too much . . . as merely symptoms of linguistic confusion'. It is not that the assertion is not both patently false, and also the product of linguistic confusion; it is both of these; but it may *also* be the product of 'linguistic penetration'. It may be that the philosopher who propounds a paradox of this sort has noticed something which is apt to be overlooked. With our present example this might be worked

ᵒut as follows: The interior angles of a plane triangle are equal
to 180 degrees—we know with certainty that that is true. Some
cats are black—we also know with certainty that that is true. So it
seems that 'The interior angles of a triangle are equal to 180°'
and 'Some cats are black' are in that respect alike. But some
people used to think that they knew with certainty that the
earth is flat; and they were mistaken. Now no doubt we *are* not
mistaken when we say that some cats are black; but it at least
makes sense to say that we *could* be mistaken, just as the flat-
earth theorists *were* mistaken. On the other hand it makes *no*
sense to say that we could be mistaken in supposing that a triangle's interior angles are equal to 180°; this *must* be true, in a
sense in which we cannot say that it must be true that some cats
are black. Thus, there is a respect in which 'Some cats are black'
is much more like 'The earth is flat' than it is like 'The interior
angles of a plane triangle are equal to 180°'; and in saying that
no empirical proposition can be known with certainty to be true,
the philosopher shows that he has been powerfully struck by this
point, which it is easy to overlook. No doubt he expresses himself absurdly, even quite mistakenly; but he does so because he
has really noticed something, and he makes us notice it too. Such
remarks, though false and confused, can be also 'illuminating . . .
when they suggest or draw attention to a terminology which reveals likenesses and differences concealed by ordinary langauge'.[1]

In short, Wisdom wishes to suggest that the sort of distortion
which lies behind, and finds expression in, the assertion of a
philosopher's paradox may be not only, as Wittgenstein would
allow, interesting and important, but also in a sense *defensible*.
The assertion itself, and the reasons given for making it, may
lead us to notice something that otherwise we might have overlooked. No doubt this result could be achieved in a less odd and
less misleading way; but there is something to be said, all the
same, for the striking power of paradox. And does not Wittgenstein himself often speak in this fashion, paradoxically?

[1] Wisdom, *Proceedings of the Aristotelian Society*, 1936–7, p. 76.

7
Categories and Dilemmas

ONE OF THE MORE important events in post-war philosophy was the publication, in 1949, of Professor Ryle's *The Concept of Mind*. Though this book preceded by four years the publication of the *Philosophical Investigations*, its general aim is entirely in harmony with Wittgenstein's ideas. Wittgenstein said that philosophical 'problems are solved, not by giving new information, but by arranging what we have always known'. Ryle similarly writes in his first paragraph that 'the philosophical arguments which constitute this book are intended not to increase what we know about minds, but to rectify the logical geography of the knowledge which we already possess'. The importance of this book derives, mostly of course from the intrinsic interest of its thesis and arguments, but partly also from the fact that it was one of the first, and hence has been one of the most widely influential, attacks in the new style upon an old family of problems. Nor is it rendered less philosophically valuable by the orderliness, clarity, and vivacity of its style, though these virtues have been thought to be dispensable, or even undesirable, by some who share broadly the same philosophical aims. Ryle has commended William James for restoring to philosophy 'that sense of the ridiculous which saves one from taking seriously everything that is said solemnly'.[1] His own book ensures that we shall not forget that, conversely, what is seriously meant need not be solemnly said.

What Ryle seeks mainly to establish is this. There is, he says, and has long been an 'official theory' about the mind, a very general doctrine or picture which has formed the background to

[1] *The Revolution in Philosophy*, Macmillan, 1956, p. 9.

almost all particular discussions in the philosophy of mind. It is Ryle's contention that this official theory, which he labels 'the dogma of the Ghost in the Machine', is not merely itself mistaken, but also has disseminated throughout this whole field a crop of interconnected and characteristic mistakes. There is need to 'rectify the logical geography' of mental concepts, not because in our ordinary transactions we find any difficulty in employing them, but because what theorists have said *about* these concepts and their employment has misguided them into a cluster of confusions; and the undetected cause of this misdirection has been the 'official theory', the unscrutinized 'dogma of the Ghost in the Machine'. In Wittgenstein's phrase, a picture has held them captive. Ryle's purpose is to break its hold, and to repair the damage it has done.

In describing the sorts of mistakes which he intends to correct Ryle makes use of a very old term which, some years before, he had himself put back into circulation[1]—namely, the term 'category'. A category-mistake,' he says, consists in 'the presentation of facts belonging to one category in the idioms appropriate to another', or in the allocation of 'concepts to logical types to which they do not belong'. The official theory of the mind, he holds, is both itself a category-mistake and a cause of countless category-mistakes elsewhere. His task is thus to correct a crop of mistakes of this sort, and to show that they derive from one, big, basic mistake which is of this sort also. Now this terminology is not, I think, wholly felicitous. It looks at first sight a good deal more precise and illuminating than it actually turns out to be, and thus has at least the deficiency of being liable to arouse expectations which are left unsatisfied. The difficulty is this, in the plainest terms: to say that some theorist has allocated some fact or concept 'to the wrong category' naturally prompts the two questions, first, to what category he has wrongly assigned it, and second, to what category it should properly be assigned. Both these natural questions presuppose, of course, that there are known and nameable categories. But in fact Ryle himself denies that this is so, and even condemns the idea that it is so with the strong word 'superstition'. He thus uses the expressions 'same category' and 'different category' without being at all prepared to say what category or which two categories are in question, and

[1] See *Proceedings of the Aristotelian Society*, 1937–8, pp. 189–206.

thus, I think, can be said to be refusing to gratify expectations naturally aroused by his own terminology. If one is not prepared, and indeed is deliberately unwilling, to say just what a category is, and what categories there are, can one really be entitled to employ the term 'category'? It is true that Ryle himself does not take this term wholly seriously. He has recently recommended it 'not for the usual reason, namely that there exists an exact, professional way of using it, in which, like a skeleton key, it will turn all our locks for us; but rather for the unusual reason that there is an inexact, amateurish way of using it in which, like a coal-hammer, it will make a satisfactory knocking noise on doors which we want opened to us'.[1] This remark, certainly, almost disarms criticism. Even so, it is not, I believe, unreasonably over-scrupulous to be ill at ease with the use of an idiom which has none at all of the precise backing which it naturally implies.

In any case it can be dispensed with. To allocate a concept to the 'wrong category' is, in actual practice, to misrepresent the use of, or to misuse, or both, the expression or expressions in the use of which that concept is applied. And this sort of misuse shows itself in two ways—in misrepresentation, first, of the ways in which expressions are related to one another, and second, of the ways in which assertions containing those expressions are validated, verified, or confirmed. Professor Ryle's contention is, then, in these terms that what he calls the 'official theory' of the mind both embodies and generates misuse, and misrepresentation of the use, of the expressions in which we speak about the mind; that these distortions generate theoretical problems and difficulties; and that *these* problems—not necessarily *all* problems—can be eliminated by the achieving of a 'clear view' of our use of this large and important department of our language.

In essence the 'official theory' as Ryle presents it hinges upon a radical bifurcation between mind and body; between physical things, events, states, and processes and mental things, events, states, and processes; between the 'external' world public to all observers, and the 'inner' life lived privately by each; between the mind, which for each of us is its own private place, and the body, which is publicly located and publicly observable in physical space. The important apparent implications of this picture are two; first, it suggests that, whereas each of us is well and perhaps

[1] *Dilemmas*, p. 9.

perfectly aware of the events that make up his own inner life, he is only deviously and perhaps not at all able to tell what goes on in the inner life of others; and second, it suggests that statements 'about the mind' differ only, but also wholly, in *subject-matter* from statements about the body—that there are physical states and mental states, bodily acts and mental acts, logically analogous, but logically independent, differing only in 'status'. These implications have raised two insoluble-seeming questions—What is the relation between the mind and the body? How can we ever know what is in another's mind?—and have produced a host of particular misconstructions of those expressions with which we refer to and talk about people's minds. They have tended everywhere to impose the idea that, if some assertion is 'about the mind', then it has simply nothing to do with the body, and vice versa; and this in turn leads to the idea that, since the bodies of others are alone observable by me, their minds must be completely inaccessible and hence unknowable. As Ryle observes, 'absolute solitude is on this showing the ineluctable destiny of the soul'.[1]

In his book Ryle predicts that his attempts to annihilate this doctrine will be misunderstood in certain ways. 'I shall probably be taken,' he says, 'to be denying well-known facts about the mental life of human beings, and my plea that I aim at doing nothing more than rectify the logic of mental-conduct concepts will probably be disallowed as mere subterfuge';[2] again, he anticipates that he will be called a behavourist. Both these charges, if charges they are, have in fact been made. But this is not, I think, due *wholly* to misunderstanding. For there could be said to remain in Ryle's book a residue, intermittently visible, of what are perhaps earlier thoughts of his own on this subject, by which these charges might well be supported. It is worth investigating how this is so.

The best general description—too general, certainly, to be very good—of Ryle's serious intentions might run as follows. He considers in turn a very large number and variety of assertions all roughly classifiable as 'about the mind'. The official theory of mind-body bifurcation tended to represent these assertions as, in the first place, logically quite unconnected with facts about the body and bodily behaviour; and, in the second place, as usually

---

[1] *The Concept of Mind* p. 15.　　　　[2] op. cit., p. 16.

referring, when in the present tense, to presently-occuring processes or events, or presently-subsisting states, in or of its supposed
'inner' theatre, the mind. Against this Ryle persistently seeks to
establish, first, that facts about the body and bodily behaviour are
nearly always relevant, and very often crucially relevant, to the
truth or falsehood of assertions 'about the mind'; and second, that
these assertions, even when in the present tense, are very often
made true or false not by anything private that is *presently* occurring or is *now* the case, but by what publicly has been or will be,
might have been or may be occurring, or the case. For example,
that Jones is intelligent is presumably an assertion about his
mind; but certainly his overt, publicly observable performances
are not irrelevant to its truth; and what assures us that it is true
or false is not something that we could (or perhaps could not)
find *now* to be the case, by inspecting his mind, but is on the
contrary our knowledge of his past performances and our estimate
of his possible performances in future. This will serve, I think,
as a painfully bald outline and example of the general respects
in which Ryle seeks, in case after case, to show that the actual
facts are at variance with the implications of the 'official theory';
and clearly he is not thereby committed to denying any well-
known facts, or to upholding any such controversial thesis as be-
haviourism.

However, there are here and there in Ryle's book some traces
of a more extreme, and in a way much simpler thesis. This is the
thesis that there *really exist* only bodies and other physical objects,
that there *really occur* only physical events or processes, and that
all statements ostensibly referring to minds are really categorical
statements about current bodily behaviour, or more commonly
hypothetical statements about possible or predicted bodily behaviour; that, hence, there is really no such thing as a private,
inner life at all, and that in principle everything about every
individual could be known by sufficiently protracted observation
of his bodily doings. It is true that even this extreme thesis might
be presented as factually neutral, as merely an 'analysis' of statements about the mind. But in fact it would be felt, and rightly,
that its real character was purely behaviouristic, and that by it
many well-known facts must be simply rejected. It cannot, I
believe, be wholly an accident that many people have believed
that Ryle's book presents this thesis. It is certainly true that he

frequently disclaims it, and very much of his detailed argument is quite free from any basis so narrow and restrictive as this. But at least this simple and over-simplifying thesis is not altogether absent from his pages. Could it be said, perhaps, to be the Ghost in *The Concept of Mind*? One may even make a guess as to what it is the ghost of; it is the ghost, perhaps, of a more old-fashioned programme of 'analysis', the attempt to reduce to some single approved grade of basic facts such propositions as seem to mention facts of other sorts. This kind of analysis, resting as it does upon a very definite dogmatic basis, is extremely unlike that species of unprejudiced investigation the sole aim of which is to achieve a clear grasp of the concepts we employ. But it seems likely that Ryle, while consciously pursuing an investigation of this latter sort, was nevertheless occasionally haunted by spectral voices from what was, after all, the very recent philosophical past. Alternatively, one might descry here and there in Ryle's copious arguments traces of an even older philosophical tradition—the tradition of ontology, of doctrines about what there really is in the universe. 'Really, there are no such things as minds; nothing really exists except bodies behaving in various ways'—certainly Ryle would not state his central contention in these terms, but nevertheless some have found passages in his book in which such an ontology has seemed to be lurking not very far behind the scenes.

There is another point at which Ryle's book has been criticized, but in this case, I think, unfairly. Ryle says that the 'official theory', the dogma, the myth of the mental ghost enclosed in the bodily machine 'hails chiefly from Descartes', though a rough genealogy might be traced further back through many theorists as far at least as Plato. Against this it has been objected,[1] in effect, that this myth or picture 'lies in our language', to use Wittgenstein's phrase—that very many of our ordinary ways of speaking and thinking, and ways of speaking also in languages other than ours, already strongly imply some such view without help or hindrance from any philosophers. This is true, no doubt; but Ryle does not deny it. What he objects to is the explicitly formulated *theory* erected on this basis, the theoretical mistakes which plain men, naturally enough, do not commonly make, but which many unwary theorists have made. It might be denied, what

[1] See, for example, S. Hampshire, *Mind*, April 1950, p. 239.

Ryle does not unqualifiedly assert, that the 'official theory' was devised mainly by Descartes; but it is surely absurd to maintain that it was not devised by any theorist at all. For theories do not formulate themselves without human aid. To find in our language many idioms suggestive of such a theory certainly entitles one to maintain that the theorists' doctrine was not arbitrary, foolish, and inexcusable. But Ryle does not suggest that it was; he claims only that it has been grossly misleading; and so, certainly, it has.

In 1954 Ryle published a little book in which he dealt with a number of separate but similar problems under the general title *Dilemmas*. The bond between the problems there discussed is a certain similarity in the ways they arise, a common feature which also accounts for their appearing as *philosophical* problems. The common feature is this. It is quite often the case that a certain kind of subject-matter, a certain field of facts or events or, in general, phenomena, can be the topic of more than one kind of inquiry, or theory, or science, or way of thinking. If so, it may happen that the conclusions or opinions on that topic arrived at in one way may seem to be in irreconcilable conflict with those arrived at in another way. We may believe, and indeed may have the best of reasons to believe, that each way of thinking is perfectly proper, and that the conclusions arrived at by each route are thoroughly well-founded; yet we still may feel ourselves obliged to think that one conclusion or set of conclusions must invalidate its rival. It is clear that this sort of intellectual *impasse* does not present us with an ordinary, departmental difficulty such as may arise *within* any theory or science or way of thinking; it is located rather on the boundaries of, or in the area between, one way of thinking and another. Its resolution, therefore, cannot be the special task of any *one* of the competing modes or systems of thought. It is in fact a task of the disentangling, straightening-out variety which is the characteristic business of philosophy.

'Dilemmas' of this general sort may differ considerably among themselves. They may be sometimes no more than puzzles, though doubtless perplexing enough as such. There is, for example, the argument of Zeno which appears to prove that Achilles in his race with the tortoise can never catch up with, let alone overtake, the tortoise which admittedly moves more slowly than he does. This conflicts with our conviction that faster runners can overhaul slower ones. But in this sort of case we do not really hesitate between the dilemma's horns. We know perfectly well that our ordinary conviction is correct, so that the problem is merely that of exposing the illusion that must lurk somewhere in the contrary argument. (In saying that the problem is *merely* this, I do not by any means wish to imply that it is easily solved.) But other cases are by no means so clear-cut as this. Professor Ryle points out, though he does not much discuss, the fact that there has sometimes been thought to be a conflict between religious or theological doctrines, and scientific theories or discoveries. In such a case as this, there would not be any general or immediate agreement that one party or the other was certainly in the right; it is not a matter merely of detecting the trick by which something we all know to be true is seemingly disproved. It is not even clear whether the apparent conflict is merely apparent, or genuine. It may be the case that the dilemma is really illusory, that when confusions are cleared away it can be seen that the apparent antagonists are not really opposed; but it may also turn out that the conflict is a genuine one, requiring that one party must yield some ground to the other. If so, the further question arises, which party must retire. Even more complex is a case of very venerable antiquity which is, however, still full of life—the case of the apparent incompatibility between the reliance we all place on the use of our senses, and scientific accounts of the processes or mechanism of sense-perception. The findings of, in particular, the neuro-physiologist have often been thought to entail that our senses cannot possibly inform us directly of the character of our environment in the way that we commonly suppose that they do, perhaps even that they cannot yield us any such information at all. It has certainly, and no doubt properly, not been thought obvious that the appearance of conflict in this case must be an illusion. Many scientists, and some philosophers, have taken it to be genuine, concluding usually, but not always, that our common convictions ought to be revised. But here there is the further complication that the horns of the dilemma are in any case not independent of one another; the evidence on which the scientific theory is founded is acquired by just that use of the ordinary senses which in the end the theory appears to condemn as unreliable. So what are we to say? Does it follow that the theory must be rejected as inconsistent, since it presupposes to be true what it also purports to disprove? Or must reliance on the senses be condemned, for the reason that to rely on them leads to the conclusion that they cannot be trusted? There are here dilemmas within a dilemma. And here Ryle says, echoing Wittgenstein's remark that his aim was 'to show the fly the way out of the fly-bottle', that 'I buzz but I do not get clear'.[1]

Long before he had come to speak in terms of categories or of dilemmas, Ryle had begun to see the tasks of philosophy very much in the way that he was later to describe in those idioms. In 1931 he had put forward the idea that 'philosophical analysis' might be 'the sole and whole function of philosophy', and that its aim was 'the detection of the sources in linguistic idioms of recurrent misconstructions and absurd theories'.[2] This observation, which says very nearly exactly the same thing as Wittgenstein was to say in his *Investigations*, at the date when it was made was advanced thinking indeed.

---

[1] *Dilemmas*, p. 92.
[2] *Systematically Misleading Expressions.* See *Logic and Language*, First Series, ed. Flew.

8

A Qualification

AT THIS POINT ONE OUGHT, I believe, to be beginning to
feel that Wittgenstein's (and Ryle's) account of philosophical
problems requires, in a certain respect, to be reconsidered. Wittgenstein at least appears to have intended his general remarks
about philosophical problems to apply to *all* such problems; his
words at any rate convey the impression that a certain generality
and exhaustiveness are claimed. This perhaps ought not to be
taken too seriously. He was, as we have said, not greatly interested
in the history of philosophy, and probably would not have wished
deliberately to assert that what every philosopher, historically
accepted as such, had actually done was what he described 'philosophers' as doing. Nevertheless, the impression of exhaustiveness
should not be allowed to stand, if one believes that it would be
substantially mistaken.

My aim at present is a limited one. In a later chapter I shall
have to describe certain kinds of inquiry which by any reasonable
test should be accepted as philosophical, but which are very different indeed from any that Wittgenstein envisaged. At the
moment I wish only to do something less than this. I wish to
raise the question whether philosophical problems, which certainly *are* of the sort that he had in view, do all *arise* in the way
that he suggested. Let us, that is, suppose for the moment at least
that in every case 'the results of philosophy are the uncovering of
one or another piece of plain nonsense'—that some philosophers
lose their way, become bewitched and bemused, and in consequence profess paradoxical or extraordinary opinions, while
other (or with luck even the same) philosophers seek, by the pro-

duction of well-chosen and well-deployed 'reminders', to defeat the enchantment and re-establish good sense. We now have to ask how this situation arises—why it is that certain theorists should thus lose their way, and give occasion to themselves or others for remedial treatment.

We have already seen something of Wittgenstein's own answer to this question: 'Philosophy is a battle against the bewitchment of our intelligence *by means of language*', against false notions 'produced by *grammatical illusions*'. But now we must consider more carefully what exactly this answer amounts to. What is meant by the expression 'by means of language'? At an earlier stage we mentioned, but did not take much care to distinguish, two rather different interpretations. There is, first, the important point that 'grammar'—or at any rate what some nowadays call 'surface-grammar', the more obvious, more literally 'formal' differences between words and expressions—is much less complex than, and hence does not reliably reflect, the many differences in actual use of words and expressions. 'Our grammar is lacking in this sort of perspicuity', as Wittgenstein observes. Hence, *particularly* in philosophy—particularly, that is, when words and expressions or the 'concepts' they represent are being, not actually used, but only thought about—there is a constant temptation to misrepresent actual uses. This may take the form of oversimplification, a failure to observe the full range or variety of uses; it may take the form, alternatively or additionally, of mistaken assimilation—of an attempt to treat some expression as resembling another in use, which in fact it resembles only grammatically. It is, I think, unquestionable that many problems have arisen and do arise in this sort of way; and I also think that one might very well describe such problems as being conjured into existence 'by means of language'. For they do not only consist, or perhaps reveal themselves, in distortions and misuses of language—that they arise at all is attributable to a feature of language itself, to the disparity, that is, between 'grammar' or linguistic 'form', and the far more complex and various uses of words and expressions. Our concepts, one might say, are more complex than our linguistic forms; our language often conceals differences, and may sometimes falsely suggest resemblances, between the concepts that we employ; and hence, though in practice we fairly seldom misuse those concepts, in philosophy we are inveterately liable to misdescribe their uses, and so to fall into conceptual entanglement.

Second, there is the matter of the power to confuse of what Wittgenstein calls 'pictures', preconceived ideas, Procrustean beds into which we may attempt with more or less intellectual discomfort to force phenomena that are really not of the right shapes and sizes. Now it might perhaps be suggested that the matter here at issue is really the same as that which we have just considered. Does not Wittgenstein say that such pictures 'lie in our language'? Does not one who attempts to assimilate 'good', say, to 'yellow' reveal himself as being under the spell of an oversimplified, preconceived 'picture' of the function of adjectives, and is not this sort of misguided assimilation precisely such as we have already admitted to be brought on 'by means of language'? Yes—but I think it is easy to see that pictures which, in this sense, 'lie in our language' are a special case of something more general. It is true that, in these particular cases, the formation of the picture or preconceived idea could plausibly be attributed to the features of language—in general, to our 'grammar' 's want of the appropriate sort of 'perspicuity'; but this is only *one* way in which a theorist may come to be damagingly saddled with a preconceived idea. There are, unfortunately, a great many others; and in most of these others it seems to me not at all appropriate to speak of the bewitchment as being worked 'by means of language'.

Let us consider an example, which might seem at first sight very conformable with Wittgenstein's view, but which in fact illustrates a large class of exceptions to it. Russell at one time propounded the typically philosophical paradox that, when for example a physiologist examines the brain of an animal, 'what the physiologist sees is in his own brain'[1]—that although one might commonly suppose that what he sees is in, or indeed *is*, the brain of the animal, this cannot be and is not in fact the case. One can see no doubt, even without any help from Moore, that something here has gone seriously wrong. Russell's dictum is hardly even paradoxical; it is simply untrue. Except in the unlikely event that the top of his skull had been removed without loss of consciousness and suitable mirrors adjusted, neither a physiologist nor anyone else would *ever* see anything in his own

[1] *An Outline of Philosophy*, 1927, p. 140.

brain. What can have led Russell into conflict with this very obvious fact?

Russell's argument runs simply enough. Perception, he rightly observes, is causally dependent upon conditions and events in the physical world. In the ordinary case in which, as I should ordinarily say, I see some object, there occurs a continuous chain of events in that object, in intervening space, in my eye, my nervous system, and my brain. Now at some point in my brain this chain of events either comes to an end, or, more probably, reverses its direction—there is set up an outgoing chain which may terminate in my making some overt 'response' to the object. At the point at which this change of direction occurs—somewhere, that is, in my own brain—is located what Russell calls a 'percept'. But this, he holds, is what I really see. For it is this that is at the inside end—*my* end—of the whole elaborate chain of events; the object itself is at the other end, is the indirect and comparatively remote *cause* of my percept. Thus the percept, which I really see, is in my own brain; and the object, which I naïvely suppose that I see, is really known to me, if at all, only by inference from that percept.

Now it is not difficult to see what has gone wrong here. Russell has deployed, no doubt correctly enough, an account of the physical conditions in which seeing occurs, and in these has picked out, justifiably, as of crucial importance a certain event in the brain. He has then spoken of a 'percept' as either identical with, or perhaps as merely located in the same place as, this crucial cerebral event; and then instead of saying, perhaps defensibly, that the occurrence of a percept is a necessary condition of my seeing something, he has said, quite wrongly, that it actually is what I see. But *why* did he make just this mistake? What 'picture' was it that was here so powerfully at work?

This question too is not difficult to answer. It seems to be almost an occupational disease of those who reflect on the human nervous system that they should picture us as somehow located inside our own heads—at the point, that is, on which all the elaborate and ramified nerves converge. The observer is represented as being confined to the centre of his own nervous system, at a point from which as it were connecting wires run out into the outside world. In that world, it appears, there occur certain events which transmit electrical impulses along these wires, and thus there occur signals at the centre of the system, at the point where the observer is imprisoned and anxiously watching. Such signals, strictly speaking, are all that he ever observes. He may be able— it is not clear how—to form some dim notion of the remote, 'external' world; conceivably, by careful inference, he may reach conclusions as to its character which stand some chance of being true. But all that he really observes is the succession of signals arriving at the inside end of his nervous network; and these, of course, are all 'in his brain'.

I imagine that this way of representing the human predicament needs only to be clearly set out to be seen to be fantastical. Our nervous systems, so far from forming a barrier between ourselves and the 'external' world, in fact put us in touch (sometimes literally) with that world in the most direct of all possible ways; and they are inside us, not we inside them. Nor need we now insist upon the numerous ways in which acceptance of this curious picture spells philosophical disaster. Our present concern is with its origin. Does it 'lie in our language'? If we allow it to drive us into flagrant absurdity, are we then deluded 'by means of language'?

Surely we are not. The bedevilling picture comes not out of language but straight—or rather twisted—from the pages of textbooks on neurophysiology, perhaps with some maleficent assistance, in this century at least, from lurking thoughts of telephone exchanges and radar-screens. The queer notion that what is seen must be in the brain certainly *results* in misinterpretation of 'our forms of language'; but it *derives* from misinterpretation, not of language, but of scientific discoveries. But why should they be misinterpreted in just this way? Why should the possession and use of a nervous system be disastrously compared, as in effect it thus is, with the possession and use of some sort of telephone exchange? This is not, we may think, hard to account for. The workings of a telephone exchange are comparatively familiar to all of us, and quite well understood; we all have a clear and tolerably accurate picture of the way in which such a system functions. Is it not then natural that the attempt should be made to understand, to explain, to render vivid and intelligible the comparatively *un*familiar workings of the nervous system by assimilating them, either overtly or by implication, to that sort of system that we already picture quite clearly? To try to make something strange look more intelligible by representing it as like something already familiar is a device that, consciously or unconsciously, we all constantly employ, often with success. The temptation to bring the same device into play in cases where in fact it leads to disaster should surely be explained as owing, not to 'the bewitchment of our intelligence by means of language', but simply to the limitations of our intelligence. We do not always think clearly; and when we fail to do so problems may arise, some of which, as in the present case, are philosophical problems.

It will be observed that the present case has in fact the form of what Professor Ryle calls a 'dilemma'. In reflecting upon what we all ordinarily say and suppose about the use of our senses, and upon what the neurophysiologist says about his own closely related topics, Russell was led to think that there was a conflict between the neurophysiologist and the rest of us—that if what he had to say was true, as there was good reason to believe that it was, then much of what the rest of us say must surely be false. It is true that he seems not to have hesitated very long between this dilemma's horns, but rather to have impaled himself without further ado upon the horn of denying what we all know quite well to be true; still, the case was one of a dilemma in Ryle's sense. Now surely such dilemmas arise, or seem to arise, as a result of some failure in clarity of thought, some conceptual confusion.[1] That this may occur is merely an instance of human fallibility. Our liability to be led into confusion 'by means of language' is certainly *one* instance of our general liability to be misled; but it is *only* one; and even if there is reason to assign to this liability a pre-eminent role in the genesis of philosophical problems, there is no case, as I have tried to show, for representing this role as not only pre-eminent, but actually unique. In so far as Wittgenstein did this—and certainly he at least appears to have done it— he was surely mistaken. The aetiology of philosophy is more various than he suggested. Even if, to return to Ryle's words of 1931, we suppose that the task of philosophical analysis consists in exposure of or opposition to 'recurrent misconstructions and absurd theories'; even if we suppose that these show themselves in

---

[1] Of course I do not imply, in saying this, that *all* dilemmas are the offspring of unclarity. Some are real enough, and loom all the more clearly for being clearly seen. But it would, I take it, be Ryle's contention that the perplexity such dilemmas generate is not typically philosophical.

linguistic, that is, in conceptual, confusion; yet we should not assume that they all have their 'sources in linguistic idioms'. I do not believe that investigation of particular problems will support any such general theory as to their origins.

9

Second Retrospect

HOW DOES THE PRACTICE of 'analysis', as that was sketched in earlier chapters, now appear, if we look back from the point we have now arrived at?

Let us consider first the case of Moore. We have described him as being characteristically concerned to do two sorts of things —first, to insist that a number of ordinary propositions, or classes of propositions, which we all very often assert or believe, are *true*, and that those philosophers who have seemed or actually intended to deny them have shown no sufficient reason for doing so; and second, to clarify those and other propositions by formulating 'analyses' of them. He has been concerned, that is, both with the 'defence of common sense', and with that clarification of thought for want of which, as he believed, 'common sense' was often outraged and high metaphysical enterprises rendered abortive.

The first of these aims, certainly, is unexceptionable. It does not of course follow, from the fact that a proposition is very generally believed, that it is certainly true and ought to be defended. No doubt there are many quite ordinary propositions of the kind miscalled 'popular fallacies'—propositions, that is, both commonly believed and false. But none of the 'truisms' that Moore defended was of this character. None of them had any concern with any recondite evidence, or could conceivably have been overturned by any startling discovery. He was concerned with only the very simplest truths about ourselves, other people, and the world we live in—truths as to which we all certainly possess the best evidence there could be and far more of it than we need. It is certain that not a few philosophers have seemed to say, or have said, things incompatible with these impregnable truisms; and a resolute refusal to abandon them, or pretend to do so, is consequently by no means pointless.

However, it could be reasonably made a complaint that Moore tended to drop this sort of question at an unsatisfactorily early stage. It is all very well to point out that some philosopher has asserted what is fantastically untrue, or has denied what is both quite certainly true and very obvious. But surely the most interesting question which then arises is, *why* he should have done this. He is presumably neither insane nor brainless. There must surely be some explanation of his curious behaviour; and would it not be of very great interest to discover how his behaviour can be explained? But in this direction Moore did very little. He looked certainly for particular errors in particular cases; but he did not attempt, as Wittgenstein did, to get to the bottom of the whole peculiar business, to explain in some reasonably general way why blatant paradox should be so *characteristic* an outcome of philosophical argument. And this was serious, for it often gave to Moore's discussions an appearance of missing the point or of begging the question. He denied, rightly, the conclusions of some philosophical arguments. But so long as the arguments themselves were left unexamined, and the motives of those who so argued left undiagnosed, the forces productive of paradox were not effectively neutralized, and the paradoxical case not properly answered. It helps little to convince me that an assertion of mine is untrue, if I am still left with the conviction that there are reasons which compel me to make it.

The case of Moore's practice of 'analysis' is rather different. Here one might say that the methods he employed were often not very well adapted to the end in view. The aim of analysis was to remove unclarity. Unclarity as to what? Not, in the ordinary sense, as to the meanings of words. We all know, and of course Moore knew that we know, what is meant by such a sentence as 'I see an ink-stand', or 'The author of *Waverley* was Scotch'. But although we all know well enough what such sentences mean, their 'depth grammar', as Wittgenstein calls it, is not at once obvious. The character of the concepts employed, their relations with other concepts, the various dimensions of presupposition and implication in their employment—all this is not obvious, and may give rise to perplexity. How then can we achieve 'a clear view' of these unobvious things? To look for an 'analysis' on Moore's pattern is to try to find some more explicit, less concentrated locution which will be logically equivalent to that to be analysed—will entail, be entailed by, and be independent of the very same things. But our language may well contain no such locution. And even if it does, can we safely suppose that to produce it will achieve all that is necessary? For at best we can clarify, by means of this sort of analysis, only the entailments, the narrowly logical features, of puzzling expressions; and may it not be that the source of perplexity lies quite outside this very limited area? To confine oneself to the pursuit of such analyses is in effect to concentrate upon, at best, only a small part of the use of our words and expressions; but the cause of our troubles may lie in our imperfect grasp of any feature of that use; there is, accordingly, no guarantee whatever that an 'analysis', even if it could be convincingly formulated, would alleviate our philosophical troubles. The most serious objection, then, to the programme of analysis is not that it is doubtful how far such analyses can be produced—though this is, in fact, quite a serious objection; it is rather that, even if they can be produced, they may well be philosophically unprofitable. What the case calls for, as one might put it, is not *definition*—not even, in Russell's phrase, definition 'in use'; it is by realistic *description*, or even, more generally still, through more explicit understanding, of use that we may hope to achieve the rational grasp of our concepts which disarms the philosophical tempter.

A good many of the same considerations apply, of course, to the programme of the Logical Atomists. But here the case is considerably complicated by the fact that they had, as Moore had not, a quite explicit mythology of language such that, if it had been true, it would have been reasonable to rely on the universal efficacy of 'analysis'. If our language had really been, as Russell thought it was, mere meat on the bones of a logical calculus; and if the calculus in question were, as it actually was, quite simply and very rigidly articulated, almost wholly independent of contextual factors, and designed for the special field of fact-stating discourse; then it *would* have been the case that most of our ordinary expressions could have been properly and even exhaustively analysed in the narrowly logical, context-neglecting manner adopted by the practitioners of 'logical analysis'. The essential task here, as Wittgenstein saw, was to bring out the extent to which this notion of the character of language was a theorists' fantasy—a case of seeming to see in the heavens a pattern that is really marked out on the lens of the telescope. Once this has been done, there is no longer any *reason* to believe in the exclusive efficacy of old-style orthodox analysis; and it can then be argued that in fact it is not necessarily, not always efficacious, on the lines already sketched out in the discussion of Moore. This course is in fact that which Wittgenstein himself had followed in his process of self-conversion in the later 1920s.

In so far as the Positivists were also committed to reliance on analysis of the orthodox pattern, much the same considerations can be applied to their case: there is no reason to suppose that the clarification of the 'vocabularies' of scientists and others, which they professed as part of their objective, can be only or best achieved in that particular way. For language is both more flexible and more various than they, in this following Russell, were accustomed to suppose. Their hostility to metaphysics raises rather different questions. On this matter I believe it would now be most effectively objected that, like Moore, they were inclined to break off at too early a point. It is laid down in effect by the Verification Principle that a (non-analytic) proposition has meaning if and only if it can, at least in principle, be verified. Suppose it to be agreed that by 'verification' is meant here some kind of empirical verification; and suppose further that the utterances of metaphysicians are found or admitted to be not susceptible of such verification. If so, then in the terms of the Principle they have no meaning. But surely the problem cannot well be left there? The Principle provides indeed an excellently brusque procedure for raising the question of the metaphysician's credentials, and perhaps it may serve really to eliminate the grosser sorts of philosophical nonsense. But in serious cases, that deserve to be taken seriously, it hardly does more than raise a question. To show that a certain metaphysical assertion is not a meaningful empirical statement is certainly to prompt the question, what then it may be; but it does not answer this question. Even if it were really the case, as in fact it is not, that non-analytic indicative sentences could be significantly employed only in making empirical statements—even if, that is, the conclusion could really

be drawn on this ground that the metaphysician's employment
of language was without significance—it would still be a matter
for serious inquiry why this sort of deviation into nonsense
should occur so persistently, and even whether, notwithstanding
its deviance and deficiencies, it might not have some significant
part to play in the history of thought. It is at just this point that
Kant's opposition to metaphysics had been much more interesting
and more effective. He had not attempted, as the Positivists did,
to explode the whole corpus of metaphysics without troubling to
wade through the works of metaphysicians. He rightly felt that it
was not enough to abuse their conclusions; their motives must be
discerned and their arguments criticized, if any real grasp of the
problems is to be achieved. It *may* be that in some sense the conclusions at which metaphysicians arrive are really without meaning; but if we are to be really rationally convinced that this is
so, it is certainly necessary to examine the works in which, if anywhere, the meaning of their conclusions will be made clear. If
one is so deeply unsympathetic to metaphysical argument that
one cannot face this prospect, one would be well advised simply
to leave metaphysics alone. Otherwise it will really be too easy to
object that one is abusing what one has not attempted to understand. The Positivists too often exposed themselves to this objection.

It might perhaps be objected here that, however ill the brisk
onslaughts of Logical Positivism may compare with the patient
subtleties of Kant, at least it cannot, surely, be said that Kant's
operations were more *effective*. For is it not evidently the case
that the type of metaphysics against which those onslaughts were
directed has, as nearly as may be, vanished from the philosophical
scene? And what effect could be greater or more striking than
that? But here there is a historical misunderstanding. The sort
of supra-mundane, transcendent metaphysics which was the particular object of Positivistic odium was, in this country, already
almost wholly extinct when their attack was launched. There was
a coffin, perhaps, to be nailed up, but no Goliath to be conquered.
The Positivists were already, as Kant in his day was not, on
the winning side.

But has there been, one may ask, a winning side at all, and
if there has, what exactly has been the scope of its victory? If it is
to be suggested that yesterday's hostility to metaphysics was at

least not conclusively pressed home, we ought to give some consideration to the present position of that subject. Is it, as some have supposed, either likely or desirable that there should be a metaphysical revival? May it be that its recent and contemporary recession has been due to no more than a change of intellectual fashions, unimportant in the longer perspective of philosophical history? These are delicate questions, and perhaps it is perilous to meddle with them. However, it would not be quite honest to pass them by.

10
Metaphysics

'PHILOSOPHY IS MANY THINGS and there is no formula
to cover them all. But if I were asked to express in one single
word what is its most essential feature I would unhesitatingly say:
vision.'—'There is something visionary about great metaphysicians as if they had the power to see beyond the horizons of their
time.'—'To say that metaphysics is nonsense *is* nonsense.'

These three quotations are taken from an article by the late
Dr. F. Waismann.[1] They certainly indicate no disposition to
regard metaphysics with contempt, as a pure waste of time, or
as the product of some fundamental misunderstanding. To do
this, he observes, would be to fail to acknowledge 'the enormous
part played at least in the past by those systems'. We ought now to
consider what part they did play—and also, why Dr. Waismann
should have been inclined to put in those qualifying words, 'at
least in the past'.

What, roughly at any rate, are we to understand by the notion
of metaphysical 'vision'? Dr. Waismann writes that 'what is
decisive is a new way of seeing and, what goes with it, the will
to transform the whole intellectual scene. This is the real thing
and everything else is subservient to it.' It is essential here, first of
all, to distinguish carefully between a new way of seeing, and
the seeing of something new. To see something new, to find
out what was not known before, is not an exercise of *metaphysical*
vision—even though the effect of this new knowledge may even
be to 'transform the whole intellectual scene'. It may be, for

---

[1] *Contemporary British Philosophy*, Third Series, 1956, pp. 447–90. Also in
Logical Positivism, ed. A. J. Ayer, pp.345–80.

example, that the theory of evolution has done as much as any-thing in the last hundred years to alter our ways of thinking, of seeing the world and our own place in it; but this of course was a scientific and not a metaphysical theory, supported not so much by arguments or would-be arguments as by an immense variety and range of empirical facts. It is by contrast characteristic of a metaphysical theory that facts should neither be cited in its sup-port nor be brought in evidence against it; it was for this reason that the Positivists were able to object that metaphysical doctrines were 'unverifiable'; such a theory consists not in an account of any new facts but in a new account of familiar facts, a new read-ing, so to speak, of what has already been agreed upon.

But do not some scientific theories still come within the scope of such a description? Certainly they do. For example, the helio-centric theory of the planetary system was of exactly this character. It offered a new 'way of seeing' astronomical phenomena without, directly at any rate, adding to astronomical knowledge; and no doubt it was for this very reason that it was thought to be of far more than parochial significance—to be, in fact a revolution-ary and even a dangerous shift in the general intellectual land-scape. However, though such theories may often be felt to be of very general, and therefore of some philosophical, importance, they themselves are certainly not metaphysical theories. Why not? Is it not because they are insufficiently general? The *direct* con-cern of the Copernican theory is solely with the movements of planets; its wider implications, if it really has any, are incidental. By contrast a metaphysical theory may be all-embracing, or im-mediately relevant at least to a very wide range of diverse pheno-mena. Such a theory as Spinoza's, for example, not only dictates a peculiar way of regarding facts in any field whatever; it was also at any rate intended to have precise moral and even religious consequences as well. It was intended to transform 'the *whole* intellectual scene', and to do this *directly,* not merely by impli-cation, or in virtue of some quirk of psychology or association of ideas. And Hegel notoriously had no doubt whatever that there was a Hegelian way of seeing *any* subject-matter, however little in certain cases he may have succeeded in conveying to others what that way was.

'Suppose that a man revolts against accepted opinion, that he feels "cramped" in its categories; a time may come when he believes, rightly or wrongly, that he has freed himself of these notions; when he has that sense of sudden growth in looking back at the prejudices which held him captive; or a time when he believes, rightly or wrongly, that he has reached a vantage point from which things can be seen to be arranged in clean and orderly patterns while difficulties of long standing dissolve as though by magic.'[1] These words describe exactly the situation of, for example, Berkeley. 'I wonder not,' he wrote, 'at my sagacity in discovering the obvious tho' amazing truth, I rather wonder at my stupid inadvertency in not finding it out before.'[2] He had the sense, as he freely asserted, of 'a vast view of things soluble hereby'. It is worth looking into his case a little further.

Berkeley was familiar, mainly through Locke, with a 'way of seeing' the world that was chiefly derived from the thriving scientific inquiries of the seventeenth century. Material things were thought of as being atomic in structure, and in character predominantly mechanical. Our knowledge of them was supposed to be founded upon the occurrence in our minds of 'ideas' caused ultimately by the mechanical operation of 'corpuscles' upon our bodily organs; and it was thought to be at least an open question how far these ideas could be regarded as reliable indications of the actual character of the 'external' world. Fundamentally the physical world was thought of as a mechanical system, describable in quantitative laws, but known to us only 'indirectly', through the mediation of sensory ideas which in some respects almost certainly misled us as to the real character of our physical environment. By this way of seeing things Berkeley felt most violently 'cramped'. It appeared to him that the interposition of 'ideas' could end only in the sceptical overthrow of our claims to any actual knowledge of the physical world. He felt that the logical conclusion of the mechanistic view must be atheism, the idea that matter was God or that there was no god at all. He could not see (and neither could Locke) how on this view the existence and immortality of the soul could be established. And in countless lesser details he thought that he found insoluble difficulties or undesirable conclusions. But then—and as it appears, quite suddenly—he came to see the whole situation differently. He changed, so to speak, his angle of vision. And at once all the

[1] Waismann, loc. cit., p. 483.
[2] *Philosophical Commentaries*, 279.

problems seemed to disappear, to be replaced by a strange but startlingly simple new picture. Suppose that matter did not exist at all! What would be the advantages of this supposition? It would simply eliminate the problems of scepticism—for then there would be no 'external world' as to which we could wonder how far our 'ideas' corresponded with it. It would utterly deflate the pretensions of physical science, the 'corpuscular philosophy' —for there would be nothing for mechanistic hypotheses to be *true* of, they would have to be presented as, at best, convenient fictions to facilitate prediction. And what would be the disadvantages? None surely—for so long as we suppose 'ideas' to occur, the course of our actual experience would be exactly the same. And does it matter that there are no longer objects to cause these ideas? On the contrary—the notion that matter could be a true cause was in any case a bad one; and now the way is clear to attribute the occurrence of ideas to their proper origin, the will of God. On this view, then, scepticism is impossible; materialism is impossible; atheism is actually self-contradictory; so far from its being questionable whether the soul exists, there in fact exists *nothing* but 'spirits and ideas'. Is there not 'a vast view of things soluble hereby'? And so far from worrying over the fact that his new view has no ordinary, gross, experimental and factual consequences, Berkeley is particularly pleased to observe that from it Common Sense 'receives no manner of disturbance'. He believed indeed that his doctrine was capable of proof; but he never for a moment supposed it to be 'verifiable'.

Here, then, is a fair example of a metaphysical theory. Almost every paragraph that Berkeley wrote was intended to amplify, to defend, to explain, to render more acceptable the 'vision' of a theocentric, immaterial universe by which he had seemed able at one stroke to escape from the difficulties and horrors of Locke's scientific, 'corpuscular', material world. 'The arguments he will offer, the attacks he will make, the suggestions he will advance are all devised for one end: to win other people over to his own way of looking at things, to change the whole climate of opinion. . . . What is decisive is that he has seen things from a new angle of vision. Compared to that everything else is secondary.'[1] He is not like a man proving theorems or relating his discoveries; he is like a reformer endeavouring to propagate a cause.

[1] Waismann, ibid.

Is there any value in such theories as these? Do such visionary projects of reform ever really succeed? It might be said that such theories may have, and often do have, the purely intrinsic value of admirable intellectual achievements; they speak well, as it were, for the capacities of the human mind; but do they ever make any actual difference? Sometimes they do—but seldom, it seems, quite the difference that their prophets intend. It appears to be most evidently true that, in its simple foundations, our ordinary 'way of seeing' the world is absolutely stable and obstinately unshakeable. Such a project as Berkeley's, which really requires us to abandon our notion of things as solid, substantial, enduring, indifferent to the presence or absence of percipient organisms, seems to attack our conceptual habits at so deep a level that it can really have no serious chance of succeeding. It is doubtful how far even Berkeley was able to retain the full sense of his vision for more than an occasional moment; one cannot so easily shake off what is natural to one's species. But we may, in other cases, come to see things differently in certain restricted fields—and really come to do so *naturally*, not in visionary moments only or in abstract theory. Dr. Waismann suggests that in the work of Descartes there may be 'a prophetic aspect of the comprehensibility of nature, a bold anticipation of what has been achieved in science at a much later date. The true successors of Descartes were those who translated the spirit of this philosophy into deeds, not Spinoza or Malebranche but Newton and the mathematical description of nature.' (Here Berkeley can be seen to have been working *against* the main trend of thought in his time.) And similarly the 'true successors' of Hegel might be said to be, not the philosophers who elaborated his doctrines into ever-deepening obscurity, but the historians whom he taught to find in the passage of time not merely a succession of independent episodes, but intelligible processes of change, of growth and decay, having certain analogies with the life-cycle of organic beings. Certainly there *may* be fields of inquiry, areas of knowledge, in which some metaphysician's new way of seeing may have the most fruitful and important results. But there may not be. His theory may stand as a mere eccentricity, with some interest perhaps, but no effect on anything whatever. Whether this will be so, he will doubtless be unable to foresee.

Why are there today few, if any, metaphysicians of this once traditional visionary variety? The answer to this question, I believe, has at least three branches. First, there have never been many real metaphysicians at any time. To be, after all, sufficiently obsessed by a visionary project of intellectual reform to spend years upon its systematization and propagation is, fortunately no doubt, a very rare condition. There may well have been in earlier times a large number of *second-hand* metaphysicians, parasitic expositors of and elaborators on the theories of some truly original figure. But such secondary labours are surely as pointless as they are usually uninteresting. Of what interest would it be to patch up, to amend and expound, the doctrines of Bradley, if really one had no inclination whatever to share the queer view from which his own fervour was derived? It is reasonable enough to abstain from such work as this; for many vastly more interesting problems lie ready to hand. Is it really surprising that most philosophers should find in these other problems their best occupation? They are fortunate today in that so very many quite unmetaphysical problems have been brought into the light.

Second, it can, I think, be reasonably said that the condition of true metaphysical fervour is today more difficult to achieve than was formerly the case; for it depends in large part upon a kind of illusion which, for good or ill and almost certainly for good, is now inevitably rare. The history of philosophy is by now a very long one; the history of the natural sciences is also pretty long, and in recent centuries has been conspicuously fast-moving and eventful. Through reflection, in both fields, on the rise, the rivalry, the decline and fall of successive systems, we have become familiar enough with the idea that phenomena may be viewed in more than one way, comprehended within more than one theory, interpreted by more than one set of explanatory concepts. It has thus become almost impossible to believe that some *one* way of seeing, some *one* sort of theory, has any exclusive claim to be the *right* way; the notion of 'reality' itself, as has commonly though not uncontroversially been held, must be given its sense in terms of some particular theory or view, so that the claim that any such theory reveals or corresponds to 'reality' can be given a circular justification which is also open, in just the same way, to quite other views as well. But the belief that some new sort of theory is merely *possible*—that some novel set of concepts or categories *could* be employed—is hardly a sufficiently dynamic incentive to engender the production of a true metaphysical theory. If one has not, and one scarcely can have, the initial conviction that a novel 'way of seeing' has some *unique* claim to acceptance, one is unlikely to undertake the considerable labour of equipping it in a full metaphysical panoply. Such work is impossible perhaps, and certainly unattractive, to the disillusioned.[1]

Further, there are no doubt in our 'climate of thought' many factors of a more general kind that are in some way unfriendly to the metaphysical temperament. One might perhaps hazard the idea that metaphysical speculation has often arisen from, and often too been a substitute for, religious or theological doctrine. If so, it could be expected to show some decline in a period when very many people neither have, nor appear to be much oppressed by the want of, any serious religious convictions. It is not obvious that, if this were so, it ought to be deplored. It is, on the other hand, quite clear how undesirable it would be for philosophers to *pretend* to suffer from cosmic anxieties by which they were in fact not seriously troubled at all. Metaphysics, like religion, ought not to be manufactured in deference to any supposed requirements of intellectual decorum, or in the pursuit of some once genuine fervour which, in present conditions, would be synthetic or simulated.

So far, in considering the nature and current prospects of 'metaphysics', I have employed that term more or less in the sense—itself, no doubt, somewhat vague—which it bore in the literature of Logical Positivism, and also in the essay of Waismann's in which he sought to expose the inadequacy of the Positivist's contemptuous dismissal of all such enterprises. There is, however, another use of the term, to be found quite clearly in Kant and perhaps to be distantly derived from Aristotle; and in this other use the term has quite recently come back into respectable currency. Kant himself used the term 'metaphysics' in two ways. First, and most frequently, he applied the term, much in the

---

[1] Some mention should be made here, as constituting a notable exception to the mood of eclectic tolerance described in the above, of the recent revitalization of 'materialism' as an ontological doctrine. I cannot do more here than refer the reader to the relevant texts, particularly to J. J. C. Smart's *Philosophy and Scientific Realism* (1963), and D. M. Armstrong's *A Materialist Theory of the Mind* (1968).

Positivist style, to the attempt to set forth, on the basis of reasoning alone, a final, comprehensive account of the ultimate nature of things; such attempts he regarded with respect, but condemned as in principle vain and illusory. But second, he occasionally used the term 'metaphysics' in speaking of his own philosophical enquiries; and here, of course, the term bore a different sense. Kant, one might say, sought to occupy a middle ground between the natural scientist and the speculative, or 'visionary', metaphysician; while dismissing as illusory the latter's attempt to discern by pure reason the ultimate nature of things, he wished also to distinguish the proper findings of philosophy from the empirical, contingent propositions of natural science. Roughly, the scientist might be regarded as seeking to establish, by experience and experiment, what is true of the world in which we live; the philosopher can and should ask, in Kant's opinion, what *must* be true of the world, if *experience* in and of the world is to be possible at all. He must ask what concepts are central in our experience of the world (whatever its actual contents may contingently be), and what conditions are necessary for the formation and application of those concepts. The task is conceptual, not experimental; but in a sense it is also descriptive, or analytical, rather than speculative. No attempt is made to establish, beyond experience, what the ultimate nature of things may be; the philosopher is rather to take our concepts as he finds them, and work out the necessary conditions of their empirical employment. This would yield what Kant sometimes called 'the metaphysic of nature'; and this Kantian enterprise is closely akin to what P. F. Strawson has called 'descriptive metaphysics'. To this matter we shall return in the chapter that follows.

11
New Questions

IT MIGHT HAVE BEEN supposed, and in fact it was sometimes said, in response to the early impact of Wittgenstein's ideas that philosophy as he represented it was, at least theoretically, a suicidal subject. It would be broadly true to say that he was interested in liberating the mind from certain cramping, rigidifying prejudices, the characteristic effect of which was to distort the course of thought in certain fields, and to produce a characteristic sense of *impasse*, a kind of helpless intellectual discontent. Certainly the earlier history of philosophy provides an enormous mass of material for just this treatment; but the supply from this source, though very large, is finite. And for the future, might not the philosophical flies become themselves so wary and enlightened as not to go into the fly-bottle at all, and hence not to need the services of any liberator? If so, though no doubt the subject might still be pursued, would it not become in a way lifeless—an exercise, instructive perhaps but rather mechanical, in exposing old modes of confusion of thought by which hardly anyone continues to be seriously perplexed? Philosophy, if so, would have shrunk to the study of its own history, with perhaps some training in specially invented puzzles for educational purposes.

It is very possible, of course, that this state of affairs would not strike anyone but professional philosophers as undesirable. But in any case it is not at all likely to come about. For one thing, the hypothesis that all serious confusions should have been dissipated and no new ones encountered can safely be proscribed as Utopian; there is no near prospect of all, or even many, philosophical heads becoming flawlessly clear. More important, however, is the fact that there are now well established within philosophy a large number and variety of questions which are not parasitic upon prior confusion. My aim in this chapter is to indicate briefly what types of questions some of these are.

Among philosophers whose main work has been done since 1945, none has been more influential, or more original, than the late J. L. Austin.[1] His manner of proceeding, which is characterized as a rule by a really astonishing minuteness and rigour, is not universally appealing, and it appears that to many its purpose is extremely obscure. However, though difficult to emulate, it is not, I believe, really hard to understand.

It is evident enough that at certain points Austin's work is quite closely related to that of Wittgenstein. It was, as we have seen, an essential feature of Wittgenstein's practice to offer 'descriptions' of our uses of language—concrete, fully-realized examples or 'reminders' of those workings of language which, in philosophy, it is so easy and even natural to misunderstand and to misrepresent. In Austin's work, too, the description of language certainly bulks large. But a closer look reveals that, in the two cases, there are marked differences both of manner and motive. The difference of manner might be partly explained as follows. It would probably be true to say that Wittgenstein was interested, both by policy and by temperament, in large, or to use his own word, 'deep' conceptual distortions; and it seems reasonable enough to suppose that a large-scale, general distortion of thought could properly be attacked by means of a comparably broad and general description of language; large prejudices demand large missiles for their due destruction. In any case Wittgenstein's own descriptions were not, as a rule, protracted or very detailed or highly systematic; they took the form more often of hints, clues, and pointers than of set exposition. It might well be held, however, that not all philosophical tangles are of this deep, almost dramatic, character. Some, and those not necessarily the least important, may originate in comparatively slight distortions and misconceptions which, in the absence of very fully detailed inspec-

[1] Austin died in 1960 at the age of forty-eight, and had published no book at that time. Since his death there have appeared his *Philosophical Papers* (1961), *Sense and Sensibilia* (1962), and his William James lectures *How to Do Things with Words* (1962).

tion of our actual language, may either escape detection altogether, or at least not be seen in their full and fell significance.
Furthermore, it could in any case well be held that the sort of
description which will yield a really 'clear view' of something so
complex as our uses of language must necessarily be lengthy and
detailed. It is then, I think, partly for just these reasons that a
prominent feature of Austin's procedure is the extreme detail in
which he examines our language, and the sharpness of his eye
and ear for very fine *nuances*.

But this difference of manner is more importantly connected,
I believe, with a difference of motive. It was certainly held by
Wittgenstein that description of language finds its whole *purpose*
in the dissolution of antecedent philosophical problems; and
hence, presumably, that it need not be further pursued than seems
necessary if that purpose is to be achieved. Austin frequently
pursued this purpose also; but it was not the only purpose that
he had in view. One might say that he believed that there is
something to be *learned*, both *from* language and *about* language,
which is worth learning whether or not we begin our researches
in the grip of antecedent confusion.

In what sense, then, are there things to be learned from language? The point here is not, I think, a mysterious or difficult one.
Suppose for example that we wish to investigate the notion of a
person's *responsibility* for his actions; we wish to know what is
contained, or how many different things are contained, within
this notion. If we then consider the language used in discussing
and assessing a man's responsibility for his actions, we find that
the available vocabulary is surprisingly extensive. On the one
hand are words like 'deliberately', 'intentionally', 'on purpose',
'knowingly', 'voluntarily'; and on the other are words like 'acci-
dentally', 'by mistake', inadvertently', 'unwittingly', involun-
tarily', 'under duress'. Now it might be thought—and indeed it
is often assumed without thinking—that this multiplicity of
ordinary idioms is unimportant; that its interest is 'merely verbal', and that the important *general* question can be adequately
discussed in terms of a simple contrast between, say, acting 'freely'
and acting 'unfreely', or between 'voluntary' and 'involuntary'
action. But to dismiss or ignore the wide variety of ordinary
idioms as being 'merely verbal' is evidently to imply that it just
happens (uninterestingly) to be the case that there is here a

number of different ways of speaking, to imply that between them there are no significant differences. But it is surely enormously unlikely that this should be so. For language does not develop in a random or inexplicable fashion. It is to be *used* for a vast number of highly important purposes; and it is at the very least unlikely that it should contain either much more, or much less, than those purposes require. If so, the existence of a number of different ways of speaking is very likely indeed to be an indication that there is a number of different things to be said; it is an indication of genuine distinctions which, if they have called into being very commonly used expressions to mark them, are not at all likely to be unimportant. It is at the same time very *un*likely that any invented, artificial, or *ad hoc* terminology will be an improvement on that which has already satisfied the most stringent of tests—that is, survival in (probably) centuries of constant actual use. Rather similarly, it is certain that there is a great deal to be learned from the immensely various everyday idioms that we find in the vocabulary of sense-perception; and much less likely that we shall be greatly assisted by terms artificially introduced by philosophers. Austin held strongly, and surely with excellent reason, that a constant, even characteristic, defect of philosophy was over-simplification, a blurring of distinctions, in the interests no doubt of ambitious generality, but actually at the price of real clarity and understanding. His practice of, as he put it, 'hounding down the *minutiae*' of ordinary language was largely directed towards revealing, with the force and freshness of real discovery, the actual complexity of the phenomena over which so many philosophers slid, with such undiscriminating rapidity, on the skates of technical terminology.

Nothing excessive is here being claimed for our ordinary language. There undoubtedly exist some areas or topics of discourse in which our everyday idioms would be of very little interest indeed; in number-theory it does not matter in the least what ordinary uses there may be of the word 'number', and in zoology we can reasonably disregard the popular use of such words as 'animal' or 'fish'. There are certainly also some recondite problems for which no ordinary vocabulary exists, and where neologism is not only justified but indispensable; psychology, for example, supplies a number of these. It was, of course, never claimed by Austin that 'ordinary language' was either all we know on earth, or all we need to know. But where the topic at issue really is one that does constantly concern most people in some practical way—as for example perception, the ascription of responsibility, or the assessment of human character and conduct—then it is certain that everyday language is as it is for some extremely good reasons; its verbal variety is certain to provide clues to important distinctions; and it is *almost* certain to be more illuminating, to work much better, than any artificial, technical vocabulary would do. In such areas languages is, as it were, a store-house of long-garnered principles and distinctions, enshrined there because they have been found important enough to merit specific linguistic recognition. If so, then on the one hand we override these distinctions at our peril; and on the other, if we wish to learn just what distinctions there are, it is to language that we can most hopefully turn for at least the beginning of an answer. Thus, Austin is concerned with our everyday language not merely, as Wittgenstein was mainly, because it serves to correct those prejudices which engender some philosophical problems, but also because it provides innumerable pointers to facts and distinctions—which might, no doubt, be arrived at in quite other ways, but less certainly, and with much more labour. His aim is not merely to describe the workings of language, but also to learn from the description— to look through it, so to speak, at the facts about the world and our concern with the world which have moulded, and continue to mould, our ways of speaking. For this purpose the description must be exact and clear; for if it is not clear and true, it will not be transparent. Words reveal nothing if we do not see them as they are. We can learn from them only if we get to know them well.

I believe that it is now possible to throw some light also on a point at which, at first sight, Austin and Wittgenstein appear to be totally opposed. It will be remembered that Wittgenstein dismissed the question 'How many kinds of sentence are there?' with the brusque observation 'There are *countless* kinds'. Austin sometimes appeared to oppose this directly—to hold that, though doubtless there are very *many* kinds, there is no reason why these kinds should not be classified and counted. But it is doubtful how far this apparent opposition is a genuine one. It is not certain that Wittgenstein meant exactly what he said. Certainly it is not clear in advance what constitutes a *kind* of sentence; and, as he says, new uses of language may sometimes crop up and others become obsolete. But equally it was not obvious in advance what should constitute a *kind* of animals; here too new kinds evolve and others die out; but we do not say simply that there are 'countless' kinds of animals; we classify them, laboriously of course, as well as we can. What Wittgenstein probably had in mind was not quite that this *could* not be done for language, but that there would be no use in doing it; and by this he would have meant that it would not advance the treatment of the type of problems which engaged his own interest. This, though not certainly true, is at least arguable. But *this*, of course, is not quite what Austin denied. He would probably, as a matter of fact, have been inclined to hold that a really thorough and well-devised classification of 'kinds of sentence' *would* have been of service even in dealing with Wittgenstein's favourite problems; but he would also, and perhaps with more confidence, have held that it would have great interest and value in itself, and would help us to learn much more from language more easily.

One purpose, certainly, which a system of classification may serve is that of *reminding* us, through acquaintance with its classificatory labels, of the variety of the phenomena within its field. It might be suggested that it is partly from the lack of any such reminder that philosophers, when they have discussed language, have concentrated overwhelmingly on just *one* kind of sentence, that, namely, in which statements are made. Against this obsessive preoccupation Austin launched a most powerful campaign. He pointed out that even grammatically indicative sentences are by no means always used in making statements; that their utterance may be proper otherwise than by being true; and 'infelicitous' in countless ways other than that of being false. He devoted very great attention to what he called 'performative utterances', their varieties and peculiar properties—utterances, frequently in the indicative mood, which have more of the character of actions than statements, which are 'operative', by the making of which something is *done*. This territory proved to be remarkably fruitful, and its exploitation powerfully disruptive of prejudices about the working of language which had long been almost instinctive in most philosophers, and damaging even in their own over-favoured field of statements.

It is in fact in this field that there survives what will perhaps prove to have been Austin's most substantial positive contribution to philosophy, in his William James lectures, delivered at Harvard in 1955, and edited for publication by J. O. Urmson in 1962. The genesis of this elaborate, though unfinished and indeed provisional investigation is to be found in his interest, mentioned above, in 'performative utterances'—in, for instance, 'I promise', to say which (in appropriate circumstances) is to promise. Austin supposed at first that such utterances were a special case—that these cases, in which to say something was to do something, to 'perform an act', could be contrasted with more ordinary cases of simple saying. But later, in the course of trying to make this contrast clearer and sharper, he came to realize that, while his original performative utterances were indeed a special case, they were not special quite in the way that he had supposed. It was not that, in those cases, to say something was to do something, for this, he now held, was true of every case; to say something is always, not just sometimes, to do something, to perform some 'speech-act'. The difference is that, in the cases he had at first considered, it is made *explicit* in the utterance what speech-act it is that the speaker is performing. This indeed is a special feature of certain utterances; more commonly, it is not to be discerned from the words alone what one who might utter those words on any particular occasion would be doing therein. But whatever is said, *some* speech-act is performed; and what Austin now required was what he called a 'general theory' of speech-acts.

There are, I believe, two respects in particular in which this angle of approach to the philosophy of language is to be valued. First, it helps to avoid the pitfalls of excessive abstraction. Speaking and writing, Austin insisted, are to be thought of first and foremost as things that people very familiarly do; the basic phenomenon, so to speak, is that of a person, in a situation characteristically involving other persons as well, performing some 'linguistic act', and the questions that fall naturally to be considered are those of what it is to perform such acts, in all their diversity, of what is needed if they are to go right, and of how they may go wrong. Words, sentences, languages, 'language' are abstractions from these actual phenomena; with 'propositions' the flight of abstraction is loftier still. Truth and falsehood, that favoured pair, are merely *among* the many ways in which utterances may go right or wrong; they are never the whole story, and sometimes are not even part of it. All this, I believe, is most salutary for philosophers to bear in mind.

The second point is this. It will be recalled from an earlier chapter that Wittgenstein gave great prominence to the idea that language is something *used*; he explicitly compared words and expressions with 'tools', and constantly emphasized (arguing against his younger self) that there are many 'uses of language'. This too was salutary; but it was also, in a sense, undiscriminating and liable to mislead; for the notion of 'use' may comprehend very many very different cases. To 'use a term differently', for example, may be to use it in a different sense, or with a different meaning; but it may also be to use it in a different way, as for instance in threatening a person as distinct from warning him; or for a different purpose, as for instance to annoy him as distinct from securing his agreement. An expression may be used jokingly, figuratively, or ironically; as a term of abuse or of compliment; in acting, telling stories, praying, or ordering groceries; to convince, to impress, to alarm, to deceive, or merely to inform. In every case we could speak of a particular 'use' of language; but it is plain that the cases are very different indeed. A difference of meaning, though it could be called a difference of use, is a very different difference from that between, say, speaking seriously and making a joke, asking a question and giving an order, or reciting a poem and making a promise—all of which also could be spoken of as 'different uses'. As a consequence of this excessive comprehensiveness of the notion of 'use', it was all too easy for those who took up with alacrity this Wittgensteinian idiom to discuss different issues without realizing that they were different, or how different they were—to describe, for instance, what a certain expression was used *in doing*, in the supposition, which at least in general is a false one, that to do this is to set out what the expression *means*. (It is a point about the use of 'bastard' that that term is applicable to illegitimate offspring, and another point that the word is often used as a term of abuse; but the former point is, and the latter is not, a point about what 'bastard' means.) Austin's interest in 'speech-acts' enabled him, I think, to see clearly the necessity for, and to begin to introduce, some crucial distinctions into this hitherto untidy territory. For, if we start from the idea that in speaking a speaker is doing something, it is really evident that there will be many different answers to the question *what* he is doing, and a consequent need to distinguish one kind of answer from another. Leaving aside what might be called non-serious, or at least non-straightforward, uses of language as in play-acting, story-telling, singing, clownish babbling, and so on, Austin was particularly concerned to distinguish (1) the act of saying certain words with a certain meaning from (2) the act of therein doing something (as making a promise, offering advice) and (3) the act of achieving something thereby (as reassuring someone, or influencing his behaviour). He called these locutionary, illocutionary, and perlocutionary acts. Though the exact grounds for and adequacy of these distinctions as he made them are matters of some controversy, that the issues raised are fruitful and illuminating is not seriously deniable.

It will be evident from all this—and even more evident to even the most casual reader of their writings—that Austin's philosophical work was very different indeed from that of Wittgenstein. I do not mean that its temperature was lower, though indeed it was, or its idiom plainer, nor merely that Austin's questions were typically much more narrowly defined than Wittgenstein's and his discussions more detailed. There were different conceptions at work of what philosophy is. Wittgenstein, as has been indicated above, had a definite view of the nature of philosophical problems; he saw them as manifestations of conceptual strains and stresses, calling not so much for answers or solutions as for elucidatory easement. Austin had no general theory of philosophy at all, no preconceptions as to the *kind* of problems philosophers might or should be confronted with; but in his own practice he wished, whatever he might have started from, to reach at some point some definite, clear, real question, and to provide for it if possible a definite, clear, and demonstrable answer. It has been said of him that his habit of mind tended to lead him out of philosophy altogether into other fields, for example into linguistics; but he would not have regarded this comment as having any unfavourable critical force. For it was, he believed, the natural end of a philosophical question to be transformed, through increasing clarity of formulation and method, into a shape in which, precisely *because* agreement on a definite solution would at last seem attainable, it would no longer strike us as typically 'philosophical'.

I turn now to comment briefly on the work of P. F. Strawson, which, original, fertile, and influential, is also in most respects markedly un-Wittgensteinian. It is evident that he has shared with Austin the belief, contrary at least to the professions of Wittgenstein, that our language is not just *unlimitedly* various and diversified, completely Protean, entirely recalcitrant to general distinction and systematization; and that it is not, in certain fundamental respects at least, at all unstable. His early work on the disputed frontiers between language and formal logic has led him, in fact, through successive stages to raise certain very general questions about language which can be seen to arise quite naturally from, but do not at all resemble, philosophical questions as Wittgenstein conceived them.

It was one of the most paradoxical, but also most admired, contentions of Russell that very many ordinary propositions, which we should naturally regard as being of the subject-predicate form, are *really* not of that form at all. According to his celebrated 'theory of descriptions',[1] most such propositions must really be understood as existential statements. In his article 'On Referring',[2] Professor Strawson first argued that this highly paradoxical doctrine could be seen to be unnecessary, if certain misconceptions were removed as to the use of expressions in referring to things. The motive for the paradox, that it, was to be removed by an accurate 'description' of that use of language which it misrepresented. A little later,[3] however, Professor Strawson went further into the question why this particular paradox should have been particularly seductive to a philosopher so much influenced by logic as Russell was; he argued that the very natural desire to assimilate language as closely as possible to a logician's calculus tended naturally to lead to neglect of 'referring' altogether, since in this use language is bound up with contextual factors in ways not paralleled in abstract calculi. However, some later logicians have argued that, though subject-predicate, 'referring' propositions admittedly *are* not, or cannot as Russell supposed be analysed as, existential statements, yet they can in theory be always eliminated and replaced by suitably framed existential

[1] See, for example, Russell, *Introduction to Mathematical Philosophy*, Chap. 16.

[2] *Mind*, July 1950. Also in *Essays in Conceptual Analysis*, ed. Flew, Macmillan, 1956.

[3] *Introduction to Logical Theory*, esp. pp. 184–90.

statements.[1] If so, the close assimilation of language to calculi might still be practicable in theory; for the troublesome involvement with context of 'referring' expressions would be in principle needless and removable. Accordingly, there now arises the general question whether this recalcitrant feature of our language *is* in theory eliminable.[2] Must there be any singular referring expressions? Or is it, as is alleged, theoretically possible that all our purposes should be served by a language which contains no such use as 'referring'? It would not be in place here to attempt to answer this question. I mention it, with some indication of how it has arisen, only as a specimen of a class of questions which are, so far at least as I can see, quite unlike any which Wittgenstein would have raised or been concerned with, and which are, though undoubtedly the proper business of philosophers, not 'philosophical' in the sense that he gave to that word.

It has been, I believe, through further reflection on these same matters that Professor Strawson has been more recently led into what he himself calls 'metaphysics' (though he importantly qualifies that noun with the adjective 'descriptive'). There is in our language, closely associated though not to be identified with the practice of 'referring', a grammarian's, and logician's, distinction between *subjects* and *predicates*: often, when something is referred to, the expression by which the reference is made will be the subject of the sentence employed, the predicate being that in which something is said of the item so referred to. Here questions arise. First one may ask, on the linguistic side, how firmly based, and on what considerations, is the subject-predicate distinction itself. One may ask whether a language *must* embody this distinction. Then, more 'metaphysically', one may turn to the objects of reference, to the particulars or 'individuals' to which subject-expressions may refer, and raise the question whether, given that we speak and think as we do, such individuals, or some of them, must *necessarily* have certain features: are there, as Professor Strawson puts it, in our conceptual system 'basic particulars', or 'primary objects of reference', which could be held, in Kantian style, to constitute a necessary feature of our

---

[1] See, e.g., Quine, *Methods of Logic*, p. 211.
[2] See, e.g., Strawson, *Individuals*, p. 194f.

conceptual equipment? In his book *Individuals*[1] he seeks to show that this basic position in all our thinking must be assigned to persons and material bodies; and this thesis, though 'descriptive' of our conceptual system rather than designedly 'revisionary' of it, can properly be said to be 'metaphysical' in one good sense—a Kantian sense—of that term.

What is perhaps particularly worth emphasizing, as a feature of the work of both Austin and Professor Strawson, is what might be called its non-negative character. Neither has embraced, or at any rate neither has rested content in, the idea that philosophy is condemned to the sole task of correcting antecedent confusion. In philosophy, as in other subjects, there are points at which we are simply ignorant, and have knowledge to acquire; there are, as in other subjects, certain straight and genuine questions to which answers, with luck or by industry or both, may be arrived at. This plain conviction, once no doubt over-confidently held, has been in some danger of total abandonment through excessive re-action. It is a matter of some importance that, with due caution, it should be re-established.

I return briefly, in conclusion, to the charge not seldom made against, in particular, Austin's investigations that they are either unimportant, or unphilosophical, or both. With the charge of unimportance it is of course difficult to deal, since it is seldom made clear by what sort of standard importance is here to be assessed. Furthermore, such questions are not easy to discuss without acrimony. The notion that Austin's inquiries do not deserve to be called 'philosophical' is, however, rather more interesting. It would of course be easy to say that it does not matter in the least what his inquiries are to be called; if some do not wish to apply to them the name of philosophy, let them by all means refrain from applying that name. But is it not, I think, at all necessary to take this short way with the question, since the employment of the name 'philosophy' can quite easily be defended.

It would, I imagine, now be generally agreed that the proper concern of philosophy is with concepts, with the ways in which and the means by which we think and communicate. It would also be generally agreed, for very obvious reasons, that this implies a concern with the uses of words. In the history of philosophy we

[1] Methuen, 1959. It is no accident that, in *The Bounds of Sense* (Methuen, 1966) Strawson has written directly and sympathetically about Kant.

find ourselves confronted, not of course exclusively, but still very frequently, with certain crucial and usually recurrent conceptual difficulties, showing themselves in, and perhaps often generated by, misconstructions or misuses or both of certain words and expressions. It is admittedly a philosophical task to understand, to correct, and thereafter if possible to avoid, these misconstructions and misuses and their attendant perplexities. On this point, I believe, there would be no disagreement. Why then, one may ask, should this negative, or curative, procedure not lead on to the positive investigation of the actual, non-distorted, non-misconstrued uses of the expressions concerned, and indeed of others? It is certainly a matter of importance to expose and to avoid the conceptual knots which have been tied in the course of centuries of philososphical argument. Why should one not then begin on the acquisition of systematic conceptual knowledge? We are for the most part extremely unclear both *what* our concepts are, and *why* they should be as they are. There is here a great deal to be found out and, if possible, explained. To hold that such investigations ought not to be undertaken, or that, if they are undertaken, they should not be called philosophy, is like maintaining that, for instance, non-clinical psychology is either a waste of time, or not really psychology. It is certainly important that attention should be devoted to relieving the psychological afflictions that occur in abnormal cases; but it would be most singular to maintain that, *unless* the relief of some affliction is the object in view, psychological research should be either not undertaken or at least renamed. One might venture indeed to continue this analogy. If psychotherapy were never to be supported by any corpus of non-clinical psychological knowledge, one would perhaps expect it to remain in a rather unhappy, jumbled, improvised, and *ad hoc* condition: if the delineation of concepts for the purpose of dispelling perplexity were never to be backed by any more detailed and systematic conceptual researches, one might well expect such delineation as occurred to be somewhat fragmentary and inadequate.

But in fact there is no need to 'expect' this; the case is before us.

12
Philosophy and Belief[1]

PHILOSOPHY IN THE PRESENT CENTURY has often been said, both by its friends and its enemies, to have undergone a 'revolution'. The questions in what this so-called revolution has consisted, what have been its effects, and whether those effects are to be lamented or not, have been widely discussed and almost inextricably confused. A few final words here will not do much, but may do something, to sort things out.

The two observations most commonly made by way of picking out the novelty in contemporary philosophy are probably, first, that it is now 'anti-metaphysical', and second, that it has become entirely 'linguistic'.

On the first of these points not much needs now to be said. It could not well support, I believe, the claim (or accusation) that a 'revolution' has occurred. For one thing, although philosophy at present is for the most part admittedly *un*metaphysical, it is not doctrinally *anti*-metaphysical in the manner of Logical Positivism; and further, as I tried to show at the beginning of this book, metaphysical writing in the style of Absolute Idealism has itself no just historical claim to the status of a tradition or an orthodoxy.[2] Russell and Moore were not wholly pursuing revolutionary new paths; they could almost as well be represented as reverting

[1] I have allowed this final chapter to stand, substantially unamended, though I do not now much like its rather acid and polemical tone. I seem to have written it, in 1958, as one conscious of encircling foes; in more recent years there have indeed been some notable onslaughts on philosophy in the tradition with which this book has been concerned, but, perhaps because they seem not to have done much damage, I would not now write, I believe, in quite so sharp, even excitable, a manner.

[2] 'Descriptive' metaphysics, in this context, is not metaphysics.

to old ones. The manner of Russell or of Professor Ayer is indeed strikingly unlike that of Bosanquet or Bradley; but it is related nearly enough to that of Mill or Hume. If what is complained of is the absence of high-flying metaphysical eloquence, then this is a complaint which could have been made of British philosophy a hundred and fifty years ago as well as today. There is here, then, no solid basis for talk of 'revolution'.

More interest, however, attaches to the proposition that contemporary philosophy has become 'linguistic'. There are some who maintain that this is simply not true, or at least that to assent to the description of philosophy as linguistic is both misleading and strategically imprudent. Sir Isaiah Berlin has said that contemporary philosophers 'have done themselves unnecessary harm, in the eyes of the uninstructed, by advertising their methods as "linguistic". No doubt this was a tempting and perhaps necessary weapon in the early days, when the current philosophical jargon—and the vast inflation of language by Hegelians and their allies—needed a sharp and immediate antidote. . . . But of course what philosophers are talking about is not words *qua* words, but about concepts and categories: the most general and pervasive among them which particular uses of words constitute (for thought is largely a matter of using words). Words are not distinguishable from the concepts they express or involve: but it does not follow that all there is before us is "mere words"—trivial questions of local usage.'[1] However, this objection to the description of current philosophy as 'linguistic' seems to amount to no more than that 'the uninstructed' may be led by that description to think ill of the subject, through drawing from it a conclusion which in fact 'does not follow'. And a desire to save the uninstructed from the consequences of their own fallacious reasoning seems hardly a sufficient motive for rejecting a description which in some sense at least is quite clearly correct. It may be true that philosophers do not as a rule talk about words '*qua* words'; but they do very often talk about words; and that they do so is certainly the most immediately obvious difference between their work and that of their predecessors. The use of the term 'linguistic' may have been 'unfortunate'; but it is also accurate enough and, one might add, candid.

[1] *The Twentieth Century*, June 1955, pp. 508–10.

But of course it is not, by itself, very informative. What is of importance after all is not the bare fact that words have come to be much discussed by philosophers, but the reason for which this has come to be so. This reason lies in new views as to the nature of the subject. Briefly, it has come to be realized more clearly than before (unless perhaps by Kant) that philosophical questions, if indeed there are any such questions, must be somehow distinguished on the one hand from questions of empirical fact, and on the other hand from formal (mathematical, logical) questions. Such questions do not arise simply through ignorance of fact, nor are they usually to be answered by deductive calculation. They arise at points where we do not 'command a clear view' of our 'concepts and categories', where in a sense we do not even see quite what the question is or, hence, how it should be approached. They may be the expression of simple perplexity—of 'the form: I don't know my way about'. They may express, more sharply, the sense of an evident 'dilemma'. Or they may give expression to a disinterested curiosity about the frequently unobvious features, whether detailed or very general, of the concepts we employ. But in all cases light is to be found, if it can be found, from a grasp of our concepts, of 'the ways in which we think and communicate'.[1] And of course, since we think and communicate predominantly in words, it follows that the uses of words must be a main topic of inquiry. That this is so does not indicate that philosophers today are concerned (though to *some* extent they are concerned) with questions quite different from those which preoccupied their predecessors; it is the effect of a new and a manifestly beneficial awareness of the character which most 'philosophical' questions have always had. It is in this respect that, in Berlin's words, 'there *has* been a great (and I should say, beneficent) revolution'. The effect of it has been to throw into new prominence discussion, not quite of the words we use, but of the ways in which we use them. And I see no good reason, if this is made clear, for much objecting to the label 'linguistic' as a mark of change.

There remains, however, a matter for controversy. There is a peculiar sense of the noun 'belief' which, for want of any ready means in English of making it intelligible, is often supplied with some sort of explanation by reference to the word *Weltanschauung*.

[1] Berlin, loc. cit., p. 510.

It may be thought, and it is, in its turn unclear what this word means. Nevertheless, the questions whether philosophy has, or should have, had at one time or ought to have had, direct relevance to questions of 'belief' in this peculiar sense have been widely canvassed, and most variously answered. They deserve some attention.

I am in fact inclined to think that, when one comes to look into these questions at all closely, they either break up or melt away to such a degree that any general statement becomes quite impossible. Let us turn first to the historical question. It may be true, in Dr. Waismann's words, that 'at the heart of any philosophy worth the name is vision'. Put otherwise, there is almost always to be found in the work of eminent philosophers of the past a characteristic 'way of seeing' such that, if in any given case one can come to understand what this typical way of seeing was, then a certain order, coherence, and intelligibility can be observed in and perhaps throughout the work of that philosopher. It could very well be argued that some such dominating vision, some characteristic way of looking at things, has been found to be a necessary condition of long-run philosophical survival. But such visions have both been, and been thought to be, exceedingly various both in their implications and in their own characters. They may, as in the case of Spinoza, be thought to entail particular religious and moral consequences; they may bear, as with Berkeley, on religion but scarcely if at all on morality; or as with Hume, on morality perhaps but on religion not at all.[1] They may be in themselves extraordinary, as in Bradley's case, or comparatively humdrum as in the case of Locke. They may derive, as with Hobbes and many others, from natural science; with Berkeley again, from opposition to science; with Descartes, from mathematics; with Russell, from logic: and in different cases the relation or relations between the 'vision' and ordinary opinions, or religion, or politics, or ethics, or aesthetics may either be, or be thought to be, or both, either intimate or remote or nonexistent. To say generally, in fact, that philosophers before the present century were directly or closely concerned with questions of 'belief' becomes quite impossible, as soon as any particular belief or kind of belief is mentioned. Were they all concerned

[1] This brief *dictum* about Hume has been warmly, and justifiably, disputed by Professor A. G. N. Flew, in his *Hume's Philosophy of Belief* (1961).

with or was their work particularly relevant to questions of religion? Certainly not. To questions of morality? In some cases only. To political questions? Comparatively seldom. Some 'vision' or other perhaps they all had. But what those visions had to do with general, non-technical issues of 'belief' is a question which cannot possibly be answered except in particular cases. The facts are to various for any quick summary.

It is, however, entirely clear that concern with very general questions of religious or moral or political belief has at no time either been or been thought to be *peculiar* to philosophers, even if the work of some philosophers, rightly or wrongly, has been adjudged to be *relevant* to such questions. There has never been any dearth of direct, non-philosophical religious, moral, and political writing. Occasionally the work of scientists has been powerfully, though doubtless indirectly, effective in these fields. And not a few novelists, dramatists, and other such persons have made matters of 'belief' their fundamental concern. Indeed there is not, I believe, any serious doubt that among the many forces which tend to shape and modify the prevailing beliefs and attitudes of societies, the influence of philosophers has been on the whole exceedingly small, and on any view is certain to remain so. Philosophers are less numerous than the clergy, less intelligible than novelists, less exciting than political pamphleteers, less revered than scientists. A philosopher who leaves the beliefs of the public alone need not fear that those questions will cease to be pursued and publicized, nor perhaps could he hope for much success if he should enter that arena. It may be in part for this reason that even those philosophers who berate the ideological neutrality of their colleagues do not themselves seem eager to tell us what we should believe, or how we should live.

I hope it may be remembered, then, that the relation of earlier philosophy to questions of *Weltanschauung* is a matter so ramified and complex that hardly anything of a very general sort can usefully be said about it. If so, this puts a large obstacle in the way of debating the question whether in this respect contemporary philosophy has changed. For what *is* this respect? Exactly what is the situation from which, if philosophy has changed, it is to be said to have departed? There really exists no antecedent position sufficiently simple and stable for philosophy today to be assessed, in relation to that position, as the same or different.

However, it is possible to venture one or two remarks, vague though the question is on which they may be supposed to bear.

It is at any rate certain that questions of 'belief'—questions of a religious, moral, political, or generally 'cosmic' variety—are seldom if at all directly dealt with in contemporary philosophy. Why is this so? The first part of an answer to this question can easily be given: there is a very large number of questions, not of that variety, which philosophers find themselves to be more interested in discussing. But many would go further. They would wish to say that philosophy has nothing to do with questions of *that* kind. Political philosophy involves the study of political concepts, but says nothing of the rights or wrongs of political issues. The moral philosopher examines the 'language of morals', but does not as such express moral judgements. The philosopher of religion may be, but by no means need be, a religious believer. They would say, more generally, that philosophy is the study of the concepts that we employ, and not of the facts, phenomena, cases, or events to which those concepts might be or are applied. To investigate the latter is to raise political or moral or religious, but not philosophical, problems or questions. It will be seen that this view is closely related to the Positivistic thesis that philosophical problems are 'syntactical', 'formal' rather than 'material'—a thesis which most would now hold to have been too narrowly formulated, but with the spirit of which a great many would be in sympathy.

From this attitude two questions may arise that should be carefully distinguished. It might be objected, first, that matters of 'belief', though indeed quite distinct from the problems now classed as philosophical, ought *also* to be made, at least more frequently, subjects of discussion among philosophers. To say simply that these matters are no part of philosophy is, it might be held, to impose an arbitrary and unreasonable restriction upon the scope of the subject, a restriction, moreover, for which there is no historical warrant. Are there not questions of a quite non-technical sort, questions about life in general and attitudes to life, which historically have been at any rate touched on by most philosophers, and which furthermore are vastly more interesting to people in general than are the highly abstract, highly 'professional', and frequently minute disputations in which philosophers currently engage?

This is not, I believe, an impressive point. No doubt one would not wish to deny that there are very vital and interesting questions of this sort. But does it follow that philosophers ought to discuss them? Have they not perhaps, like physicists or philologists, their own special and specialized concerns in which in fact, for what the point is worth, they are evidently more interested? Is it really any use exhorting or instructing them to do something else? Their position after all is not usually such that they have any great interest in pleasing the public or pursuing mass audiences; they would not be much put out if those whom their work did not attract should pay simply no further attention to it. Even if, as in fact is not perfectly clear, their present concerns are somewhat more confined than the concerns of philosophers historically have been, it is not clearly improper nor in the least degree unusual for such progressive specialization to occur. Finally, is it certain that those philosophers who have dealt largely in *Weltanschauung* have done so to any great purpose or profit? And could it be any more certain that, if those questions were now to be more frequently mooted among philosophers, the outcome would be particularly valuable? A marked capacity for abstract thought is compatible with an 'attitude to life' entirely ordinary, or even dull. A philosopher's views in this area might be expected to be consistent and reasonably clear; but they might well, while fulfilling those conditions, be absolutely uninteresting. If so, one need not complain if he should keep them to himself.

But second, some philosophers, conscious perhaps of the lack of weight in this first objection, have raised a rather similar point in a more telling form. The view that philosophy is, to repeat an expression employed just now, ideologically neutral is held widely enough for it to be becoming increasingly fashionable to deny it.[1] The fashionable objection is that current philosophical views and procedures are *not* distinct from, unrelated to, matters of the *Weltanschauung* variety; so that for philosophers to disclaim any concern with those matters amounts in fact to their being blind to the implications of their practices. The suggestion is not that

[1] Alternatively, to take it to be true of contemporary practice, and to offer what are meant to be condemnatory sociological explanations of that circumstance. Such enterprises, I believe, are really too purely speculative to be of very much interest.

questions of a different kind should be admitted within the scope of philosophy, but that those questions necessarily are within its scope already and therefore ought not to be, as they often are, passed over in silence. Discussion of this important suggestion has suffered, unfortunately, from extreme imprecision. Points have been made on either side of extreme generality and quite indeterminate effect. It has been said in support of the suggestion, truly enough, that some religious and even some political authorities have seen in contemporary philosophy implications sufficiently grave and substantial to merit suspicion or open hostility; could this be so, if the subject were ideologically neutral? But to this it can easily be replied that those authorities have perhaps not understood the character of their adversary; may they not be oppressed by implications which are not really there? It may then be urged on the other side that philosophers themselves actually exhibit a quite striking ideological range—politically from left to right, in religion from Roman Catholicism to atheism, in morality from puritanism to marked un-rigour; yet broadly the same sort of philosophical practice appears to be compatible with any of these positions. To this in turn it can be not absurdly replied that perhaps, underlying these apparent gross differences, there may be some deep-seated similarity of attitude and outlook, in which it may be that future historians will find without difficulty the *Weltanschauung* of contemporary philosophy. What is certainly lacking is any *demonstration* of the ways, if any, in which current philosophy has such general implications, to set against the undeniably plausible *prima facie* contention that it has none. However, this might be attributed to the difficulty of becoming aware, at any given time, of the deepest, most unquestioned presuppositions of the day. If so, it would appear to be the course of prudence to await with due humility the verdict of history.

It is in any case a rather curious fact that philosophy in general should be made so often a target for public complaint or criticism. There are after all a great many academic subjects in which, as they are at present pursued, the general public neither finds nor could well be expected to find any sort of interest. Yet no one is moved to complain of this state of affairs, or to urge the professors of those subjects to turn their hands to matters that would engage the concern of a wider audience. Why are philosophers not thus allowed to go their own way? No doubt there are many reasons. But one, I think, is this. There is a sense in which philosophy has only rather recently achieved professional status. This has occurred in two ways. First, 'where Mill, Huxley, and Leslie Stephen had published their articles in the ordinary reviews, Bradley, Moore, and Russell published theirs in the philosophers' professional organ or in the Proceedings of the philosophers' metropolitan forum. This new professional practice of submitting problems and arguments to the expert criticism of fellow craftsmen led to a growing concern with questions of philosophical technique and a growing passion for ratiocinative rigour. Eloquence will not silence rival experts and edification is not palatable to colleagues. . . . Philosophers had now to be philosophers' philosophers; and in their colloquia there was as little room for party politics as there is in courts of law.'[1] Second, it is only quite recently that the subject-matter, or rather the tasks, of philosophy have come to be clearly distinguished from those of other disciplines. In this way too, connected of course with the other, the subject has not long been standing firmly on its own feet in its own territory. For these reasons I believe that philosophy has not yet been accepted as a subject which its practitioners should be left to practice. There lingers a certain sense of the old, kind days of amateurism, the days, as it were, when anyone could join in, could have his own say, and could expect to be listened to. Those who have not moved into, or have moved out of, professional circles have, perhaps, still a sense of a certain deprivation, a vague feeling that the total amateur ought not to be disqualified from engaging in what was, so recently, an amateurish pursuit. (I believe that the position of literary criticism is here very similar.) On the professional side too there is perhaps a certain nostalgia. The old amateurs were occasionally conspicuous public men. Their cogitations were of interest to, and rightly or wrongly were thought to be of importance in, far wider circles than would now be likely to be reached by even the most admirable of contributions to philosophy. Thus, perhaps, it comes about that certain philosophers deplore the present aspect of their own subject, and that, more commonly, certain non-philosophers discuss philosophy with a plaintive and patronizing impertinence which they would not dream of displaying towards any other

[1] Ryle, *The Revolution in Philosophy*, Introduction, p. 4.

subject in which they were admittedly ill qualified. There is not much need to worry about this. The present state of affairs is doubtless temporary and transitional; and in the meantime the complaints that are made are quite certain to be ineffective.

For my own part I am inclined to think that they only need feel strongly hostile to contemporary philosophy who have cause to fear or to dislike a clear intellectual air and a low temperature of argument. It seems to be true that the contemporary philosopher's eye is characteristically cold and his pen, perhaps, apt to be employed as an instrument of deflation. It is largely for this reason that, however narrowly technical, however refined and minute and even pedantic, the pursuits of philosophers may be or may become, any age or society in which those pursuits were wholly neglected would be, in my judgement, seriously the worse for that. In our own case we have, at present, no ground for apprehension.

Bibliography

1. *Books:*

I have included in the following list, apart from some of the more important writings of philosophers discussed or mentioned in the text, a small number of other recent and contemporary works which seem to me to be either valuable in themselves, or representative of the periods in which they were written, or both.

BRADLEY, F. H. *Appearance and Reality*, Oxford, 1893.
EWING, A. C. *Idealism, A Critical Survey*, London, 1936.
WOLLHEIM, R. *F. H. Bradley*, London, 1959.
MOORE, G. E. *Philosophical Studies*, London, 1922.
—— *Some Main Problems of Philosophy*, London, 1953.
—— *Philosophical Papers*, London, 1959.
—— *The Commonplace Book, 1919-53*, ed. C. Lewy, London and New York, 1963.
—— *Lectures on Philosophy*, ed. C. Lewy, London and New York, 1966.
WHITE, A. R. *G. E. Moore: A Critical Exposition*, Oxford, 1958.
RUSSELL, Bertrand *Philosophical Essays*, London, 1910.
—— *The Problems of Philosophy*, London, 1912.
—— *Our Knowledge of the External World*, London, 1914.
—— *Mysticism and Logic*, London, 1918.
—— *Introduction to Mathematical Philosophy*, London, 1919.
—— *The Analysis of Mind*, London, 1921.
—— *An Inquiry into Meaning and Truth*, London, 1940.
—— *Human Knowledge*, London and New York, 1948.

—— *Logic and Knowledge*, ed. R. C. Marsh, London and New York, 1956.

—— *My Philosophical Development*, London and New York, 1959.

URMSON, J. O. *Philosophical Analysis*, Oxford and New York, 1956.

PEARS, D. F. *Bertrand Russell and the British Tradition in Philosophy*, London and New York, 1967.

BROAD, C. D. *Scientific Thought*, London, 1923.

LEWIS, C. I. *Mind and the World Order*, New York, 1929.

RAMSEY, F. P. *The Foundations of Mathematics*, London, 1931.

CARNAP, R. *Logical Syntax of Language*, London, New York, 1937.

—— *Introduction to Semantics*, Cambridge, Mass., 1942.

—— *Meaning and Necessity*, Chicago, 1947.

WEINBERG, J. K. *An Examination of Logical Positivism*, London, New York, 1936.

POPPER, K. R. *The Logic of Scientific Discovery*, London and New York, 1959.

WITTGENSTEIN, L. *Tractatus Logico-Philosophicus*, trans. C. K. Ogden, London, 1922; trans. D. F. Pears and B. F. McGuinness, London, 1961.

—— *Philosophical Investigations*, Oxford, 1953.

—— *Remarks on the Foundations of Mathematics*, Oxford, 1956.

—— *The Blue and Brown Books*, Oxford and New York, 1958.

—— *Notebooks 1914-16*, Oxford, 1961.

—— *Zettel*, Oxford, 1967.

ANSCOMBE, G. E. M. *Introduction to Wittgenstein's 'Tractatus'*, London, 1959.

GRIFFIN, J. *Wittgenstein's Logical Atomism*, Oxford, 1964.

BLACK, M. *A Companion to Wittgenstein's 'Tractatus'*, Ithaca, N.Y., 1964.

PITCHER, G. W. *The Philosophy of Wittgenstein*, Englewood Cliffs, N.J., 1964.

RYLE, G. *The Concept of Mind*, London, 1949; New York, 1950.

—— *Dilemmas*, Cambridge, 1953; New York, 1954.

PRICE, H. H. *Perception*, London, 1932.

—— *Thinking and Experience*, London, 1953.

AYER, A. J. *Language, Truth, and Logic*, London and New York, 1936.

—— *The Foundations of Empirical Knowledge*, London and New York, 1940.

—— *Philosophical Essays*, London and New York, 1954.

—— *The Problem of Knowledge*, London and New York, 1956.

—— *The Concept of a Person*, London and New York, 1963.

WISDOM, John, *Other Minds*, Oxford, 1952.

—— *Philosophy and Psychoanalysis*, Oxford, 1953.

QUINE, W. V. O. *Methods of Logic*, Cambridge, Mass., 1951.

—— *From a Logical Point of View*, Cambridge, Mass., 1953.

—— *Word and Object*, New York, 1960.

HAMPSHIRE, S. *Thought and Action*, London, 1959; New York, 1960.

AUSTIN, J. L. *Philosophical Papers*, Oxford and New York, 1961.

—— *Sense and Sensibilia*, Oxford and New York, 1962.

—— *How to Do Things with Words*, Oxford and New York, 1962.

STRAWSON, P. F. *An Introduction to Logical Theory*, London, 1952.

—— *Individuals*, London, 1959.

—— *The Bounds of Sense*, London and New York, 1966.

ZIFF, P. *Semantic Analysis*, Ithaca, N.Y., 1960.

WAISMANN, F. *The Principles of Linguistic Philosophy*, London and New York, 1965.

11. *Collections:*

In recent years collections of articles, specially written or reprinted from periodicals, have appeared in almost unmanageably large numbers. I list below a few such collections, with absolutely no attempt to achieve completeness.

Readings in Philosophical Analysis, ed. H. Feigl and W. Sellars, New York, 1949.

Philosophical Analysis, ed. M. Black, Ithaca, N.Y., 1950.

Logic and Language, First Series, ed. A. Flew, Oxford, 1952; New York, 1956.

Logic and Language, Second Series, ed. A. Flew, Oxford and New York, 1953.

Essays in Conceptual Analysis, ed. A. Flew, London and New York, 1956.

Contemporary British Philosophy, Third Series, ed. H. D. Lewis, London, 1956.

The Revolution in Philosophy, ed. D. F. Pears, London, 1956.

The Nature of Metaphysics, ed. D. F. Pears, London and New York, 1957.

British Philosophy in the Mid-century, ed. C. A. Mace, London, 1957.

Logical Positivism, ed. A. J. Ayer, Glencoe, Ill., 1959.

Philosophy and Ordinary Language, ed. C. E. Caton, Urbana, Ill., 1963.

Truth, ed. G. W. Pitcher, Englewood Cliffs, N.J., 1964.

Ordinary Language, ed, V. C. Chappell, Englewood Cliffs, N.J. 1964.

Perceiving, Sensing, and Knowing, ed. R. Swartz, New York, 1965.

Brain and Mind, ed. J. R. Smythies, London and New York, 1965.

British Analytical Philosophy, ed. B. A. O. Williams and A. C. Montefiore, London, 1966.

The Linguistic Turn, ed. R. Rorty, Chicago and London, 1967.

The Philosophy of Perception, ed. G. J. Warnock, Oxford, 1967.

Philosophical Logic, ed. P. F. Strawson, Oxford, 1967.

Knowledge and Belief, ed. A. P. Griffiths, Oxford, 1967.

The Philosophy of Action, ed. A. R. White, Oxford, 1968.

The Theory of Meaning. ed. G. H. R. Parkinson, Oxford, 1968.

(The last five volumes form part of the series 'Oxford Readings in Philosophy', published by the Clarendon Press, Oxford.)

There should also be mentioned three volumes in the 'Library of Living Philosophers' series, namely:

The Philosophy of G. E. Moore, ed P. A. Schilpp, Evanston, Ill., 1942.

The Philosophy of Bertrand Russell, ed. P. A. Schilpp, Evanston, Ill., 1942.

The Philosophy of Rudolph Carnap, ed. P. A. Schilpp, La Salle, Ill., and Cambridge, 1963.

J. Passmore's *A Hundred Years of Philosophy*, 2nd edn. (London and New York, 1966) deals comprehensively with, among much else, a good deal of the subject-matter of the present book. See also A. M. Quinton, 'Contemporary British Philosophy', in *A Critical History of Western Philosophy*, ed. O'Connor, Glencoe, Ill., 1964.

Index